TABLE OF CONTENTS

P9-DWT-316

PAGE

Editor

Richard P. Keeling
CEO & Executive Consultant
Keeling & Associates, LLC

Contributing Authors

Robert Bonfiglio
Vice President for Student Affairs
SUNY College at Geneseo

Susan E. Borrego
Vice President for Student Affairs
California State University, Monterey Bay

Gwendolyn Jordan Dungy
Executive Director
NASPA–Student Affairs Administrators in Higher Education

Cynthia S. Forrest
President and Consultant
Cynthia S. Forrest & Associates, Inc.

Jane Fried
Professor
Central Connecticut State University

Gail Short Hanson
Vice President of Campus Life
American University

Susan Komives
Associate Professor
University of Maryland, College Park

Richard Mullendore
Professor and Doctoral Program Coordinator
University of Georgia

Gregory Roberts
Executive Director
ACPA–College Student Educators International

Sarah Schoper
Graduate Student
University of Maryland, College Park

Jacqueline D. Skinner
Director of Educational Programs
ACPA–College Student Educators International

Jeanne Steffes
Associate Vice President for Student Affairs
Syracuse University

LEARNING RECONSIDERED 2:
Implementing a Campus-Wide Focus On the Student Experience

American College Personnel Association
Association of College and University Housing Officers–International
Association of College Unions–International
National Academic Advising Association
National Association for Campus Activities
National Association of Student Personnel Administrators
National Intramural-Recreational Sports Association

Richard P. Keeling, M.D.
Editor

Learning Reconsidered 2: Implementing a Campus-Wide Focus on the Student Experience

Copyright © 2006 by the American College Personnel Association (ACPA), Association of College and University Housing Officers–International (ACUHO-I), Association of College Unions–International (ACUI), National Academic Advising Association (NACADA), National Association for Campus Activities (NACA), National Association of Student Personnel Administrators (NASPA), and National Intramural-Recreational Sports Association (NIRSA).

ISBN 0-931654-41-6

PARTNER ASSOCIATIONS

ASSOCIATION OF COLLEGE UNIONS INTERNATIONAL (ACUI)

Founded in 1914, ACUI is a nonprofit educational organization that brings together college union and student activities professionals from hundreds of schools in seven countries. Its members work on urban and rural campuses, in two-year and four-year institutions, and at large and small schools. They are students and administrators whose mission is to build campus community. ACUI enriches them all through education, advocacy, and the delivery of services. www.acui.org

COLLEGE STUDENT EDUCATORS INTERNATIONAL (ACPA)

Founded in 1924, ACPA–College Students Educators International is a comprehensive student affairs association that seeks to involve professionals and educators through its programs and services. ACPA is the professional home for over 8,000 members from more than 1,600 colleges and universities nationally and internationally. In the area of learning, ACPA provides institutes, online learning, workshops, and an Annual Convention. The Association also publishes *About Campus* magazine and the *Journal of College Student Development*, which are distributed to faculty, administrators, and institutional libraries. The association also has philanthropic support from the ACPA Educational Leadership Foundation. www.myacpa.org

ASSOCIATION OF COLLEGE AND UNIVERSITY HOUSING OFFICERS– INTERNATIONAL (ACUHO-I)

ACUHO-I is the preeminent professional association dedicated to supporting and promoting the collegiate residential experience by: creating value through services, information, and collegial relationships that are indispensable to its members; and continually changing and adapting in ways that assist members in meeting the needs of dynamic campus environments. www.acuho-i.org

NATIONAL ASSOCIATION FOR CAMPUS ACTIVITIES (NACA)

NACA links the higher education and entertainment communities in a business and learning partnership, creating educational and business opportunities for its school and professional members. Established in 1960 to help increase the buying power of campus programming dollars, NACA now has more than 1,050 college and university members and more than 600 associate members who represent artists, lecturers and performers. Today, NACA offers a wide variety of events, educational workshops, publications, Webinars and networking opportunities for colleges and universities across the country. NACA's programs focus on program planning, risk management, multicultural education, concert management, student and professional leadership development, student government and more. Through its Web site, www.naca.org, NACA also provides students and professional staff with a number of online programming and professional development tools. www.naca.org

THE NATIONAL ACADEMIC ADVISING ASSOCIATION (NACADA)

NACADA is the leader within the global education community for the theory, delivery, application, and advancement of academic advising to enhance student learning and development. NACADA's 9,000-plus members throughout the United States, Canada, and numerous other countries strive to ensure student success. NACADA champions the role of academic advising to enhance student learning and development, addresses the academic advising needs of higher education, advances the body of knowledge on academic advising, and affirms the role of academic advising in supporting institutional mission and vitality. http://www.nacada.ksu.edu

NATIONAL ASSOCIATION OF STUDENT PERSONNEL ADMINISTRATORS (NASPA)

NASPA–Student Affairs Administrators in Higher Education is the leading voice for student affairs administration, policy and practice and affirms the commitment of student affairs to educating the whole student and integrating student life and learning. NASPA has more than 10,000 members at 1,400 campuses, and represents 29 countries. NASPA members are student affairs administrators, faculty, and graduate students who serve a variety of functions and roles including the vice president and dean for student life as well as professionals working within housing and residence life, student unions, student activities, counseling, career development, orientation, enrollment management, racial and ethnic minority support services, and retention and assessment. www.naspa.org

NATIONAL INTRAMURAL-RECREATIONAL SPORTS ASSOCIATION (NIRSA)

NIRSA is the leading resource for professional and student development, education, and research in collegiate recreational sports. Headquartered in Corvallis, Ore., NIRSA was established in 1950 at a meeting of 22 African-American men and women from 11 Historically Black Colleges and Universities at Dillard University. NIRSA now includes nearly 4,000 highly trained professional, student and associate members throughout the United States, Canada and other countries. NIRSA members serve an estimated 5.5 million students who regularly participate in campus recreational sports programs, and they are actively engaged in many areas of campus life: student leadership, development, and personnel management; wellness and fitness programs; intramural sports; sport clubs; recreation facility operations; outdoor recreation; informal recreation; and aquatic programs. www.nirsa.org

INTRODUCTION

Richard P. Keeling

From the beginning, *Learning Reconsidered* linked ideas to practice. The extended title—*A Campus-Wide Focus on the Student Experience*—held the idea of reconsidering learning close to the ground and reminded us that it is, after all, students and their experience that give meaning and purpose to our work. In our need to put things in categories, we have classified some parts of higher education as curricular, and other parts as co-curricular, but students just call it college. From its initial statement of purpose ("... to re-examine some widely accepted ideas about conventional teaching and learning, and to question whether current organizational patterns in higher education support student learning in today's environment") to the final quotation on the endpaper ("The most important factor is that transformative learning always occurs in the active context of students' lives"), *Learning Reconsidered* was a doggedly practical document, intended for use in the active context of the lives and work of practitioners.

The warm reception it received must surely have been generated in part by that characteristic. But just as important must have been the emphasis that *Learning Reconsidered* maintained—which was on student affairs as a partner in the broader campus curriculum and the ways in which the work of student affairs affects student outcomes, rather than on student affairs qua student affairs, the profession itself. *Learning Reconsidered* understood and addressed student affairs in the active context of academic life, recognizing that the transformation of higher education would occur there, and nowhere else.

Now we have *Learning Reconsidered 2*, with an extended title modified only by the addition of the word "implementing." *Learning Reconsidered 2* works, like its predecessor, in the active context of academic life. It amplifies the original publication in two ways: first, by reporting the actual experience of student affairs educators who have developed and assessed learning outcomes, found points of collaboration across campus, or identified new ways to link their work to learning activities, and second, by exploring in greater depth how the ideas and concepts in *Learning Reconsidered* can support all campus educators in finding ways to use all the resources in the education and preparation of the whole student.

The chapters in this volume deepen our engagement with student learning (rethinking learning, mapping the campus learning environment, developing student outcomes) and broaden the territory explored (strategic planning, internal assessment, professional development, collaboration). Many of them—and, notably, all of Chapter 10—provide specific examples of actual experience. With seven associations joined as partners, the volume of material submitted far exceeded the space constraints of an affordable publication. The good news is that there is a wealth of additional material—templates, case studies, program examples—that could not be included in this document. Even better is this news: that there will soon be a Web-based version of *Learning Reconsidered 2*; rather than being a recapitulation of the printed document, it will have its own separate structure and character, and will include a far greater number of examples, resources, and reports.

For simplicity, we have used the name *Learning Reconsidered* throughout the document to refer to the original publication (2002).

Gwen Dungy, executive director of NASPA, Greg Roberts, executive director of ACPA, and I, as editor for this second volume, extend our warm thanks to the authors and to the many professionals from ACUHO-I, ACUI, NACA, NACADA, and

NIRSA who contributed to the richness and texture of the ideas and examples represented. Their work is more obvious in some chapters than others, but every chapter benefited from their comments, suggestions, and experience.

CHAPTER 1
LEARNING RECONSIDERED: WHERE HAVE WE COME? WHERE ARE WE GOING?

Gwendolyn Jordan Dungy

Learning Reconsidered was born from the idea of shared responsibility for student learning. It both responded to and complemented *Greater Expectations: A New Vision for Learning as a Nation Goes to College,* the report of a national panel convened by the Association of American Colleges and Universities (Greater Expectations National Panel, 2002). *Greater Expectations,* released in 2002, called for improvements in the quality of student learning and challenged higher education to provide a practical liberal education that would prepare students for life, work, and civic participation in an increasingly complex world. It asked anew some fundamental questions: What will be the role of higher education in the future? What should students be learning in college? What are good practices in a learning-centered academy?

Greater Expectations called for the integration of traditionally disparate elements of the curriculum—general education, the major, and electives. It was clear to NASPA, however, that the quality of educational experience and outcomes advocated in *Greater Expectations* would require the broad participation, contributions, and commitment of all campus educators—notably including student affairs professionals—and that the integration of learning must embrace out-of-classroom experiences as well as all aspects of the formal academic curriculum. But student affairs educators wanted a blueprint to guide their work and explain how it could intentionally enhance the quality of learning and the student experience.

Learning Reconsidered: A Campus-Wide Focus on the Student Experience (now called *Learning Reconsidered*) became that blueprint. The document was provided in three versions—a longer scholarly edition suitable for use in graduate education, a monograph now widely distributed in print and available for download as a .pdf document, and a brief brochure for audiences outside higher education. It deliberately linked to the spirit of *Greater Expectations,* it reemphasized the tenets of ACPA's *Student Learning Imperative* (American College Personnel Association, 1994); it connected back to the initiatives and actions recommended in the ACPA and NASPA document, *Principles of Good Practice* (American College Personnel Association and National Association of Student Personnel Administrators, 1997) and it renewed the commitment to collaboration advanced in the joint publication of AAHE, ACPA, and NASPA, *Powerful Partnerships: A Shared Responsibility for Learning* (American Association of Higher Education et al, 1998). Because *Learning Reconsidered* would speak broadly of the shared work of supporting student learning, it needed a strong foundation in the entire profession of student affairs, so NASPA and ACPA worked in partnership to create and disseminate it. But it was never intended to be— and never became—simply another report talking to student affairs about student affairs. Instead, it is a seminal document about the nature of, responsibility for, and outcomes of learning at the beginning of the 21st century.

HOW *LEARNING RECONSIDERED* IS BEING USED

More than 10,000 copies of *Learning Reconsidered: A Campus-Wide Focus on the Student Experience* are in circulation on college and university campuses worldwide. The document has been used as an invitation from student affairs educators to their colleagues in other sectors of their institutions to engage in dialogue and planning for institution-wide student learning outcomes. It has become a frequent focus of professional development programs and workshops, and is the topic of many presentations at regional and national conferences of student affairs associations. Many educators are using it in conjunction with *Greater Expectations* to show how their curriculum, courses, or experiential learning activities will promote specific learning outcomes.

WHY *LEARNING RECONSIDERED 2*?

Introduced at the NASPA and ACPA annual conferences in March 2004, *Learning Reconsidered: A Campus-Wide Focus on the Student Experience* elicited an enthusiastic response that has been sustained through more than two years of discussion, debate, conference presentations, and professional development workshops. The most common request in response to the document has been of this type: Now that we have definitively stated that transformative learning always occurs in the active context of students' lives and that the work of student affairs is integral to all learning and not just developmental in nature, how do we create the dialogue, tools, and materials to implement the recommendations?

This need for practical assistance harkens back to the original working title of *Learning Reconsidered*, which was: *A Blueprint for Action.* Student affairs educators agree with the concepts; now, they want to implement the recommendations.

They have learned that changing the culture of a campus to one that supports the intentional development of institutional learning outcomes *before* the creation of programs and interventions is difficult. They want to demonstrate that there must be an assessment of quality and value—in terms of student learning—in every program and activity. They want to know how to challenge the structures and language of learning—to move beyond ideas of separate learning inside and outside the classroom.

Those questions were the impetus for the preparation of *Learning Reconsidered 2: Implementing a Campus-Wide Focus on the Student Experience.* Jeanne Steffes, President of ACPA, re-convened the original authors early in 2005 to begin to outline a follow-up document that would provide practical assistance to student affairs educators who wanted to use the ideas of *Learning Reconsidered* in their programs, services, and activities. To make the work as helpful and relevant to as many professionals in the broad field of student affairs as possible, NASPA and ACPA brought several other associations into the process of writing *Learning Reconsidered 2*:

- Association of College and University Housing Officers–International (ACUHO-I)
- Association of College Unions–International (ACUI)
- National Association of Campus Activities (NACA)
- National Academic Advising Association (NACADA)
- National Intramural and Recreational Sports Association (NIRSA)

The value of this broad partnership is realized in the comprehensiveness and practicality of *Learning Reconsidered 2.*

CHAPTER 2
RETHINKING LEARNING

Jane Fried

WHY RECONSIDER LEARNING?

Learning is fundamental to living and is, of course, the reason for higher education. But there are good reasons to rethink our ideas about learning—how it happens, what supports it, and what its outcomes are. The way in which we define and understand learning is critical to our effectiveness in working with students and professional colleagues. If our definitions or understandings are inaccurate or out of date, our ability to work with students and faculty colleagues may be impaired as well.

- **Our model of learning is out of date and inaccurate.** In the academy, teaching has usually been understood as the transfer of information, and learning as the ability to acquire, recall, and repeat information. People who knew information explained it to people who did not know; anyone who could repeat what they had been taught or demonstrate their mastery of the material in some other way was considered to have learned. This teaching/learning model continues to prevail, with technological modifications, in our modern institutions; lecturing remains a key mode of teaching, despite the widespread availability of information from multiple printed and electronic sources. One must wonder why it is still the norm to believe that repeating information for students to transcribe is a productive educational activity. While faculty lecture, technologically-astute students may wonder if it is possible to download the contents of a relevant Web site directly into their brains

without writing anything down. There is a serious disconnect between the ways in which students are used to learning about their world, the ways in which knowledge is made available outside the classroom, and the ways in which we are still "teaching" and defining learning. There are at least two other components of learning that are equally or more important in today's world: *intellectual understanding* and *making intellectual and practical sense of experience* (Caine, Caine, McClintic & Klimek, 2005, p.2). The processes for stimulating these additional types of learning are situated in parts of the brain that are not normally involved in memorization or the mechanical repetition of material.

- **Our ideas about learning are embedded in a *positivist epistemology*.** This means that we typically do not address personal questions of meaning, experience, or involvement in learning. Our ideas about learning have historically been shaped by the belief that knowledge exists objectively, separate from the person who is learning: learning can be considered a process of apprehending information and retaining it. But even in the domain of scientific knowledge, where positivism is most widely accepted, the notion of a separation between the knower and the known fell into disrepute early in the 20th century when Heisenberg articulated the uncertainty principle (for a more detailed discussion of positivism as an approach to learning, see *Shifting Paradigms in Student Affairs* [Fried & associates, 1995]). Learning within a positivist epistemology does not address questions of personal meaning or knowledge construction. It leaves the construction of meaning to the learner and places it outside the academic learning process.

- **The construction of meaning no longer occurs only in the academic context.** This split between knowing and creating meaning has become more significant because of changes in the demographics, purposes, and assumptions of students. When college attendance was limited to a relatively small percentage of the population and most students were single, lived in residence halls, and focused their lives on campus with peers, there were often opportunities and time outside classrooms to think about the meaning of things and to discuss ideas with friends. Although knowing information and organizing knowledge into meaningful patterns that could be applied in one's life did not necessarily occur in the same place on campus, these activities did occur in the same time frame.

But the financial and time pressures of modern life have changed the pace, the amount of time students devote to studying, and both their ability and willingness to think about the meaning of what they are learning. Finding a better job or developing one's own career possibilities rank at the top of the list of reasons for college attendance. Developing a meaningful philosophy of life has not been prominent as a reason for college attendance since the 1960's. This instrumentalist orientation to college attendance can easily become the death knell for general education requirements, which have provided one of the last opportunities to create a sense of personal meaning in the context of higher education. And in our current era of postmodern, deconstructivist challenges to classic beliefs, we can assume no broad consensus about

the meaning of things or the creation of personal identity (Anderson, 1997; Foucalt, 1970; Foucalt, 1980). There is therefore a great deal of current interest in student spiritual development and in the processes by which students construct meaning in their lives (Baxter Magolda, 1999; Miller & Ryan, 2001; Parks, 2000).

- **Constructivism: a challenge to positivism.** An alternative epistemological and pedagogical approach to teaching and learning called *constructivism* addresses the issues of construction of meaning, the roles of self in society, and the ways in which context shapes perception and relationships (hooks, 1994; hooks, 2003; Friere, 1990; Giroux, 1992). Constructivism assumes that meaning emerges from inquiry, knowledge acquisition, and the relationships and conversations among people who learn. It also acknowledges that individual perspective and life experience shape each person's interpretation of information. Constructivism challenges positivism in a profound way by asserting that there is rarely a single truth about any situation although there may be a consensus about accurate information. Constructivism is widely practiced in some disciplines, but may be a new concept to many other educators.

Nevertheless, constructivism tends to shape our ways of doing things and thinking about our work (Argyris, 1982); we are all constructivists to the degree that we realize that every story has two sides, that in most situations it is impossible to tell "what really happened," and that, most of the time, what really happened is not as important as what the participants in the situation believe happened or how they interpret what happened. As educators, we might find that an understanding of constructivism would enable us to develop a common language that would facilitate the development of partnerships and collegial relationships with members of the faculty.

WHAT HAVE WE LEARNED ABOUT LEARNING?

Learning Reconsidered: A Campus-Wide Focus on the Student Experience ("Learning Reconsidered") defines learning as "a complex, holistic, multicentric activity that occurs throughout and across the college experience" (American College Personnel Association and National Association of Student Personnel Administrators, 2004, p.5). We have learned that:

- **Learning has physiological, social and emotional, cognitive, and developmental dimensions.** All brains are organized in slightly different ways, but most people need to find patterns and meaning in what they are learning. Active, experiential learning followed by cognitive processing in emotionally safe environments produces extremely powerful, or transformative, learning. On the other hand, fear inhibits learning and undermines increases in cognitive complexity (Caine, Caine, McClintic & Klimek, 2005).

- **Learning is characterized by a flowing process in which students acquire, analyze, and place information into a pre-existing pattern of meaning, often expanding or altering that pattern.** A particularly significant aspect of this process is the creation of one's own identity; rather than a static idea or experience, identity has been re-conceptualized as a process of individual consciousness in context, with an inner, relatively consistent set of core perspectives and beliefs and numerous external interactions with the social and physical environment that influence or shape identity in particular settings.

- **It is impossible to separate learning, development, and context** (Jones & McEwen, 2000; Abes & Jones, 2004). If learning is an integrated process, we can help students learn in far more powerful ways by integrating our approaches to learning opportunities regardless of their location on or off campus. The integration of learning requires mapping of the campus and identifying learning goals. Both of these subjects are discussed in greater detail in other chapters.

- **Powerful learning transforms how students view themselves and the world.** Transformative learning increases students' ability to think about the world, themselves, and how they think and learn. Mezirow calls this process "learning to think like an adult" (2000, p.3) or "the process of using a prior interpretation to construe a new interpretation of the meaning of one's experience as a guide to future action" (p.5). Kegan differentiates between informative learning and transformative learning: "Informative learning changes what we know; transformative learning changes how we know" (2000, p.50). In the 21st century, all educated people must understand and manage their own learning processes because of the need to continue learning.

Our understanding of learning needs and processes must deepen as we design new methods of helping people learn. As institutions transform themselves to focus on learning, the ways in which teaching is conducted and learning opportunities are delivered must also change. All of these changes should be informed by knowledge of two on-going trends: 1) increased awareness of the physiology and psychology of learning, and 2) increased awareness of the various contexts in which new learning will be applied (Dolence & Norris, 1995).

SOME ELEMENTS OF THE PSYCHOPHYSIOLOGY OF LEARNING

All transformative learning involves the learner as a whole being—body, mind, emotion and spirit. This type of learning is anchored in many centers of the brain, all of which interact with each other as the process occurs. "Aha!" moments of learning occur when the various elements form a coherent pattern that yields insight for the learner and is reflected in measurable brain wave phenomena (Zohar, 1990).

It is certainly not necessary to understand all the elements of brain functioning to learn to design and evaluate transformative learning. Learning must occur in several modalities and locations that are integrated with regard to moving the student toward the achievement of a learning goal that can be assessed. Transformative learning is very likely to occur if a student is engaged in experiences that:

1. Are challenging, but not threatening, such as computer games or simulations,

2. Are complex and designed to demonstrate a process or phenomenon clearly,

3. Provide the opportunity to process the experience verbally, either in writing or in conversation,

4. Expect the student to describe what the learning means personally, in the context of his or her life experience, and

5. Allow enough time to reflect on all of those questions.

Designing learning experiences with the potential to provoke transformation and assessing learning outcomes is similar to learning to drive a car. You have to know where to put the key, how to steer, and when to put in gas and change the oil, but you don't have to know how the engine runs or how to do a computer diagnostic test on the electrical system.

CAMPUS LEARNING SYSTEMS

Learning Reconsidered contains a "map" of a campus as a learning system. The student is at the center of the system as a person who engages in behavior, makes meaning of experiences and new information and uses cognition and affect to engage the environment. Meaning-making processes are critical for transformative learning. Students move through social, academic, and institutional contexts—in both "real" and electronic forms—attending classes, eating meals, hanging out with friends, participating in activities, talking with faculty members, paying bills, using the library, playing games, meeting with an academic or career advisor, and, for fewer than 20 percent of current students, using his or her room in a residence hall. All of these contexts provide opportunities for students to learn, some by design and some because of events that occur spontaneously. Every campus will map these opportunities differently and use these processes in slightly different ways; Borrego, in Chapter 3, explicates this process in relation to key factors, such as institutional mission and campus culture. In this complex set of learning environments, we need to learn how to write learning goals and assess learning outcomes in many different settings and then develop templates by which assessments can be framed in a common language of learning.

LEARNING GOALS AND LEARNING OUTCOMES

Every academic course has learning goals and outcomes, some more explicitly stated than others. For example, a composition course might include a learning goal that students will be able to construct a five page essay, presenting two different points of view, comparing and contrasting those viewpoints and presenting evidence for both sides of the issue, and writing a balanced conclusion. Using an evaluation rubric or set of standard expectations for a particular skill, the instructor can assess the student's level of achievement for the learning goal at the beginning and end of the course. During the course, the same rubric can be the basis for feedback to students about their progress.

Setting learning goals and assessing outcomes for the goals identified in *Learning Reconsidered* is considerably more complicated. Such goals are typical of the general education requirements of many institutions, goals to which the entire institution is committed but for which no particular department may be responsible. For example, California State University at Monterey Bay has University learning requirements that include community participation, culture and equity, democratic participation, English and mathematics communication, ethics and vibrancy (see www.csumb.edu). These are the types of goals that, when achieved, provoke transformation in awareness and affect development, perspective, and worldview. Efforts to achieve or inspire progress toward the achievement of these goals must be embedded in the entire environment in an integrated way so that students are aware of the concrete and practical dimensions of goal achievement, and

able to identify numerous places in their lives where progress can be made toward achievement. The goals must be written in such a way that learning sites and opportunities are identified, outcomes are described and assessment procedures are made clear. Assessment should be used as a feedback loop to tell students how they are doing and where they need to continue to improve.

Jernstadt (2004) suggests that knowledge is acquired and used on a continuum and that learning is most effective if it incorporates many modes of learning in many contexts. His continuum of learning is *knowledge, recognition, application and extrapolation.* The chart below suggests ways of thinking about the location of different learning functions (adapted by Fried as a handout, 2004)

Whatever the learning goals for a particular process might be, the acquisition, application and extrapolation of knowledge is best learned by what Jernstadt calls "target practice" (personal communication). Students must be able to articulate what type of learning is important; then they need to practice learning, and be able to demonstrate their mastery of goals, in a variety of environments.

Chart 1
Learning Functions

Classroom functions	Life purposes and opportunities
1. To know (principles)	1. To apply and analyze
2. To recognize the skills and knowledge that are appropriate in different situations.	2. To test, evaluate and rethink
3. To extrapolate and imagine	3. To evaluate and imagine again
4. To discuss and examine from many perspectives	4. To reconsider in the light of personal values, construction of meaning, self-authorship, family priorities and needs.

Source: Fried, adapted from Jernstadt (2004).

EXAMPLES

On a practical level, setting learning goals and assessing outcomes is a systematic process. Campuses can develop their own templates for the process or borrow from preexisting ones.

Civic engagement can serve as an example for the construction of a template. What does civic engagement mean as a learning goal?

- Students must be able to *understand and describe* the machinery of civic entities—learning how decisions are made in the public domain, how elections work, what various commissions and committees do, how the government functions and interacts with citizens. This kind of learning occurs in political science classes, in student government, and through service learning or attendance at public hearings, to name just a few venues.

- Students must also be able to *understand and analyze the consequences of community participation in civic decision-making*. This goal can be achieved by reading and discussion of case studies in which communities became involved in changing the circumstances of their environments, such as the garbage workers' strike in Memphis, Tenn., that Reverend Martin Luther King, Jr. was supporting when he was assassinated. There are numerous anthropological and journalistic accounts of all kinds of community engagement that document change when citizens became actively involved.

- Finally, students must *demonstrate civic engagement* themselves and reflect on the experience from personal, political and philosophical levels. Students can demonstrate engagement though involvement in student government, the governance of any other organization to which they belong, attendance at public hearing, tracking the progress of some civic initiative in the local

news and discussing it with peers, writing letters to the editor, holding open discussions on campus and inviting civic leaders and so on. For all of these activities, students must be required to reflect—generally, to write about what they have learned and to identify the knowledge and skills they have developed as a result. There should be opportunities for them to place this learning in the larger context of their own lives so that they can describe what it all means to them and how these experiences contributed to their own sense of self-authorship.

In template format, the general goals would appear as follows, with specific items to be added for each campus:

- Students will be able to explain . . .

- Students will seek out opportunities to learn . . .

- Students will demonstrate the skills of . . .

- Students will be able to analyze . . .

The template should also identify what opportunities will be provided for students to explain how the learning experience affected their identity and the roles they might play in communities while in college and beyond.

A recent guide to writing learning outcomes is *Understanding by Design* by Wiggins and McTighe (2002), which is accompanied by an extensive workbook filled with examples of learning goals, design processes and means of assessing learning outcomes. Unfortunately for the profession of student affairs, all the guides to defining and assessing learning outcomes are written for classroom teachers, most of them for K-12 populations. The gap between designing training, which most student affairs professionals are thoroughly familiar with, and designing other learning experiences is not wide, but it requires different skills. Wiggins and McTighe (2002) suggest that templates be constructed by using these steps:

1. Identify desired results—knowledge, context, big ideas, enduring understandings and transfer of learning;

2. Determine acceptable evidence—through performance of what authentic tasks will students demonstrate success? What other evidence will support this demonstration (e.g., journals, tests, discussions)?

3. Design appropriate learning experiences and instruction—what will students do in order to learn designated skills and knowledge, and be able to apply them to real life situations?

CONCLUSION

Our profession is continuing on the journey that was first articulated by Esther Lloyd-Jones in *Student Personnel Work as Deeper Teaching* (1940). One of our many roles in our relationships with students is to help them learn in both practical and theoretical ways and to develop knowledge and skills that will help them in their life journeys. The skills that students need today are somewhat different than they were in the middle of the 20th century, particularly in the domains of life-long learning, turning knowledge into wisdom, and developing cross-cultural skills. Nevertheless, we have always helped students learn in real life settings and helped them reflect on the meaning of what they have learned in the context of their own lives. We simply have not paid a great deal of attention to our role as learning facilitators nor have we developed the language to describe what we are doing in teaching/learning terminology. Now is the time to expand our vocabularies and deepen our relationships with faculty colleagues; we must collaborate with all educators on our campuses to articulate what our students are learning.

CHAPTER 3
MAPPING THE LEARNING ENVIRONMENT

Susan E. Borrego

INTRODUCTION

Anne Sullivan, the successful teacher of Helen Keller, provides a great example of understanding that the potential for learning exists in a variety of forms and activities. Keller was blind, deaf, mute and initially unresponsive to the efforts of the teacher. Shoelaces, sunshine, water, food, language—Sullivan understood that her role as teacher was to be intentional about utilizing day-to-day activities for learning. As we map learning environments and explore opportunities that exist in the academic, social and institutional contexts of our campuses, it is important to remember that the potential for learning is limited only by our imagination. As educators we have remarkable opportunities to create environments that will engage students in richer and broader learning.

Throughout their campus experience, students move through its social, academic and institutional environments. Students interact with each other and with faculty and other educators; they participate on athletic and debate teams; sometimes they live in campus housing; they study in groups, collaborate in club activities and organizations, establish relationships, work out, possibly commute to campus, often work part-time in a campus or community job, and sometimes manage families. All of these aspects of students' lives provide opportunities for learning. Learning happens as students develop competencies by designing student activities, participating in service learning, or gaining experience through student employment. They acquire knowledge and integrate it with their experience in leadership programs, community service, and student government activities. They learn about themselves when an event fails, when they struggle to work with others who are different from them, or when they experience the success of a group project. Students are empowered as they navigate campus financial aid and academic support systems.

Whether we are working inside or outside the classroom, overseeing student employees or teaching in a classroom or laboratory, most of us have observed students making the connections between something they were doing in our classes or programs and their own prior experiences. Typically, students say that these "Aha!" moments help them make sense of their lives in the broad sense, rather than subject by subject or experience by experience. The more practitioners understand how learning happens (see Chapter 2) and develop the ability to map the campus to mine opportunities for learning, the more likely student affairs educators will influence the campus toward deeper student learning experiences.

The critical assumption guiding this chapter is that the entire campus is a learning community.

The process of mapping learning opportunities is relatively intuitive for practitioners. This chapter provides some guidelines for that process.

FIRST STEPS IN MAPPING THE LEARNING ENVIRONMENT

Mapping a learning environment is the process of recognizing, identifying, and documenting the sites for learning activities on campus; it provides the framework within which student affairs educators can link their programs and activities to learning opportunities. It is leveraging our programs and resources in ways that promote opportunities to deepen student learning. Fresh collaborations for learning are realized by focusing on creating learning outcomes that support student success. A campus committed to engaging members in new paradigms of learning, practicing new pedagogies, and creating experiences to support learning must be truly "learner-centered." This means that all campus educators (both faculty and student affairs professionals) must review and consider changing their practice. Mapping an environment informs practitioners about the kinds of activities that will enhance classroom experiences and help the campus develop a broader understanding of transformative learning.

Immediately after beginning my work as an administrator on a primarily residential campus, I realized that the conversations about student learning only embraced credit-bearing courses. Even service learning only qualified as learning if a student served off-campus and was enrolled for credit. Peer mentor programs, peer health education training, student leadership activities, work as residence assistants, and experiential learning activities were not included in the campus discussion about student learning. Consequently, these programs were not allocated adequate resources. Over time, the campus culture had come to define learning as "academic learning"—and to map all learning, in effect, to classrooms and laboratories.

As discussions began about renewing the strategic plan, I was able to introduce a conversation about the larger scope of student learning that included activities like the ones listed earlier. We began to talk about institution-wide student learning outcomes; that discussion set the stage for more in-depth conversations about strengthening the campus learning community. The current budget process is reexamining what kinds of activities are needed to support learning across campus. Engaging the community in conversations about student learning and student success provided a new dimension for the strategic planning process.

Because learning has been traditionally defined in separate curricular and co-curricular terms, the challenge to successful mapping for a more holistic student experience is to shift our own language and practice and look to institutional learning outcomes as the basis for our interventions and programs. In the absence of specific institutionally-defined learning outcomes, *Learning Reconsidered* proposes general outcomes that are larger than the classroom and address the aspects of a whole, learner-centered experience.

Questions like these drive the process of mapping the learning environment:

- What is the mission of the campus?

- What are the campus' learning objectives or outcomes?

- How does the work of student affairs support those outcomes?

- What new opportunities might arise when one asks first, "What is the intended outcome?" and *then* "What programs or services can be organized to support that outcome?"

- How can one create interventions in light of understanding that learning happens in multiple dimensions across the campus environment?

MISSION INFLUENCES THE MAP

The next step is to understand what gets counted as learning in a particular environment. The mission of an institution greatly influences the type of programs and activities that count as learning. The mission will also help you understand what motivates the students and faculty as you design programs and leverage activities and events in ways that will support the learning outcomes of the campus and enhance students' experience.

As will be described in Chapter 4, a variety of factors have led to a more intentional focus on learning outcomes. Commitments to engaging the learner as a whole person, moving from teaching-centered models to learner-centered ones, and providing evidence that students are learning from multiple sources on a campus all drive the work of creating a fluid learning environment. But different campuses have different emphases, based on different missions. The educational focus of a liberal arts campus is different than a research-based campus. Further, what motivates the learners and potential collaborators may also be quite different.

On some campuses there may be very little explicit value in broad outcomes such as practical competence or civic engagement. But, rather than dispensing with such outcomes, we can adapt them within the context of the mission. Two examples follow:

1. At one research-based campus, the "coin of the realm" was laboratory experience. A critical aspect of the student's academic success was to get involved in lab groups and have experience working in a lab. While this was not within the purview of student affairs on the campus, student affairs professionals were responsible for the summer "bridge" program, and student affairs educators were able to work with faculty and students to design a lab learning experience that would develop practical research competence.

2. At a large land grant university, leveraging learning activities in academic programs with the resources in student activities led to new interventions that maximized student learning. Campus dining services, the student activities office, the food studies program, and the university union collaborated to provide a lunchtime healthy food series. For six weeks, student chefs prepared healthy meals, providing free samples to students. Campus dining services donated the equipment and had their chefs on hand to assist, and student activities donated bags of groceries to be raffled off so students could take home the ingredients and recipes of the meals that had been prepared. The student chefs got to practice and the student observers learned about healthy meal options. The program required no new resources; it simply made better use of existing ones.

Successfully supporting student learning requires an understanding of the type of learning the campus aspires to and values. Being able to identify opportunities for engaged, integrated learning is an important skill for student affairs practitioners. It is essential to know how best to position programs so they support learning outcomes of the institution.

LEARNING OUTCOMES FOCUS THE MAP

Developing our learning outcomes in line with institutional outcomes and priorities embeds the work of student affairs in student learning. Every program should have clear and specific learning outcomes and a clear link to the mission of the campus (or its institutional learning outcomes).

Some student affairs practitioners have argued that the process of establishing and documenting student outcomes interferes with our traditional services, especially in auxiliary operations. But the rationale for most services in student affairs is to advance learning. Students who successfully navigate the financial aid system, for example, develop practical competence, increase their inter/intrapersonal competence, and enhance their academic achievement. Auxiliaries on our campuses are often staffed with large numbers of student workers; these workers are seldom seen as leaders and they are seldom trained beyond the specific function they are providing. But, as the examples given in Chapter 10 will show, there are abundant opportunities for using student employment in campus services and auxiliary operations as the substrate for a deeper learning experience.

Every event or activity needs specified learning outcomes. There are numerous stories from our colleagues in student affairs about faculty who will not show up for events outside the classroom. But too often student affairs professionals make "cold calls" inviting faculty to dinners, sports events, or field trips; all without clear goals identified for their participation or student learning. Faculty members talk about being invited to events with low student turnout, no student affairs staff onsite, or no clear idea about what they were supposed to do at the event. The job of a practitioner is to organize events around learning, and the success of the event is measured by the resulting change in students' abilities, skills, or ways of thinking as opposed to the number of people who attended. One example of a successful faculty/student affairs event that meets those criteria is a brown-bag series where faculty shared their research.

While student affairs practitioners support student learning with specific programs and activities, we also support student learning by delivering services that smooth the student's path on campus and keep obstacles out of the way of learning. Part of our role is to provide effective services so that students do not focus on service problems. Health and counseling services, advocacy and intervention services for students with disabilities, and programs that support minority students are all examples of student affairs interventions that support learning by removing or modifying barriers. Helping to make this connection more explicit on campus will emphasize the contributions of student affairs services to student learning and better define the roles of student affairs practitioners. Engaged pedagogy is not necessarily a new skill for practitioners; however, describing our work in the context of learning outcomes or student learning *is*.

RELATIONSHIPS MAKE THE MAP COME ALIVE

Margaret Wheatley (1999), a distinguished consultant on organizational change, observes that where organizational change has been realized, it has been as a result of successful relationships.

Similarly, successful learning happens in relationship—relationships with new ideas, new people, and new ways of achieving.

Student affairs professionals are positioned to host the relationships that maximize student learning. In mapping the learning environment, identifying key relationships is critical. A colleague in student activities described a project that created excellent opportunities for students, built powerful relationships with art faculty, and drew a great deal of attention to both the art department and the programs the activities director was creating. He needed posters designed for a speakers series and had a very limited budget. He offered a small stipend and a place in which students' poster designs could be displayed.

What evolved was a marketing internship program that gave students practical experience, developed a set of relationships with faculty that were important to the director in a larger context, and resulted in an opportunity to provide a learning experience for students and celebrate student achievement. Once each semester, faculty and student affairs educators met with students to give academic feedback and describe market response. The director received his posters, the learning community maximized resources, the students carried out a practical, rewarding assignment, the faculty members achieved their objectives, and everybody learned.

Intramural and recreational sports professionals report that faculty members teaching foreign languages have sought to use space in recreation centers for language classes; the class activity is to play volleyball, or another sport, while using only the language being studied. Recreation professionals create and host the specific learning environment, support the work of the faculty member, and help make athletic activity a learning event. Opportunities are often missed because we are not looking broadly enough for ways to maximize student learning.

MAPPING REMINDS US TO TAKE CUES FROM CAMPUS CULTURE

Seeing and utilizing the entire campus as a learning community is often difficult for important reasons. Many of us are products of the very educational systems that we are trying to critique. While we talk often about multiple perspectives, evolving pedagogies, or reconsidering learning, our practice remains rooted in familiar, traditional customs. To map a learning environment successfully, we have to be willing to examine our own assumptions about what we think will work and pay attention to the cues of those around us.

- Several years ago I worked at a highly selective science institute. The curriculum was rigorous, the culture very specific, and the interests of faculty and students were largely about the work of science. My professional pivot foot was planted in student learning so I began to look for ways to deliver services and create programs that would support an intensive research-based model of learning.

  I facilitated an AIDS 101 workshop, and the first year brought a panel of people living with AIDS to talk with students. This was an approach that I had successfully used on several different campuses. With this audience it simply did not work. The students asked questions relating to the biology and the science of the illness. There was little discussion about the quality of life of panelists or personal safety and education.

  At the end of the session, as I was debriefing with the panel, one of the panelists pointed out that he had never been in this kind of a situation: "This group needs a doctor or a scientist." The next year I organized a session that was facilitated by a physician who was an AIDS researcher. He spent the first 30 minutes talking about the science of AIDS and then connected it to issues of living with AIDS. The doctor facilitated the panel and closed with a discussion about the prospects for an HIV/AIDS vaccine and the need for healthy and safe choices. It was a more

successful educational program for everyone involved.

- A second opportunity on that campus involved a summer bridge program. The program had morphed several times over a period of 10 years, and no one was happy with it; students felt it didn't prepare them well, faculty were frustrated with the delivery of curriculum by non-faculty, and parents believed the program marked their students as "remedial." In fact, although none of the students participating were there for remedial reasons, the campus viewed the program as remedial.

  As I began to meet with groups interested in the program, a new model began to emerge. Several students had been part of an academic preparation program they thought would adapt very well to this campus. The faculty was engaged by conversation about orienting students to a research-based model of education as opposed to the more traditional teaching-based model students had experienced in high school. Ultimately, the redesign of the program proved successful and faculty, student affairs, and students formed stronger relationships. We developed an experiential activity familiar to student affairs practitioners but rooted in science and mathematics. This program illustrated how student affairs professionals, taking cues from campus culture, can design successful programs that support student learning.

CONCLUSION

Mapping the campus is not new to most practitioners, but it has typically not been clearly defined and documented. Unfortunately, therefore, student affairs practitioners have often been outside the conversation about learning on campus. Before service learning became institutionalized and credit bearing, student affairs educators were developing ways to train student leaders through experiential education activities such as wilderness trips, adventure programs, "urban plunges," and ropes courses. Student affairs practitioners were collaborating with faculty in residential living/learning communities, developing opportunities for students to practice skills of leadership, communication, self-awareness, and self-agency.

The work of engaging students is not new to the profession. As we expand our understanding of learning and how it happens, we will be able to work with the faculty, using a common language, to develop more integrated learning experiences. Identifying ways in which our programs integrate with the learning outcomes of an institution will provide opportunities for enhanced student learning. Understanding how learning happens and exploring that in the context of the particular setting of our work is critical to our ability to support learning across campus.

CHAPTER 4
DEVELOPING LEARNING OUTCOMES

Susan R. Komives

Sarah Schoper

INTRODUCTION

The story is told of the city slicker who gets off the train in a small mountain town. He notices a youth down the street who is taking pot shots with a BB gun at various targets (the side of a barn, a picket fence, and a stop sign). The youth then walks up to the target and appears to study the shot, and moves on. Approaching the first target, the visitor is impressed to note that the shot is dead center in the middle of a bull's eye. The same is true with each target! He catches up with the youngster and says, "Young lady, I am very impressed with your shooting. How did you learn to shoot that well?" She pauses a moment and says, "Aw, shucks, it ain't nothing. I shoot first and draw a circle around the hole later."

That story leads us to ask what changes would occur in our work—and, indeed, across our institutions—if we were to identify the target first (i.e., specify desired, intended outcomes), and then design programs, strategies, and other college experiences that would contribute to those outcomes. This chapter will explore the context of the outcomes movement, describe the kinds of learning outcomes sought in higher education, and suggest techniques to assist your department, division, or entire campus focus on identifying and designating outcomes.

THE STUDENT OUTCOMES MOVEMENT
IN CONTEXT

The growing and vibrant interest in student outcomes (often called student learning outcomes)

is the product of thought and action in several converging themes over the past 20 years. Understanding the convergence of these interconnected themes illustrates the complexity of this new emphasis.

1. **Reform movements.** Reform movements in higher education are closely linked to antecedent movements toward reform in K-12 education. After the publication of *A Nation at Risk* (1983)—the report that asked "Why can't Johnny Read?"—the 1980's were filled with a series of higher education reform reports intended to examine and exhort post-secondary education to revisit its overall mission, examine general education, reframe institutional mission, reaffirm campus community, respond to growing diversity, and identify and assess outcomes. Reports such as *Involvement in Learning,* the Carnegie Commission's report *College (1987),* and *Reclaiming a Legacy* documented the need for reform.

2. **Student Learning Movement.** In the 1980's many reform reports admonished higher education to return to a focus on undergraduate education and the importance of quality teaching. Although many institutions had never deviated from that commitment, and indeed many considered it their primary purpose, large research universities enrolling most of the nation's students were perceived as having strayed away from it. Barr and Tagg's widely read *Change* magazine article, "From Teaching

to Learning," (1995) further nudged thinking away from a teaching paradigm (it is not all about the faculty) to a learning paradigm (it is about students). Reform reports in the 1990s—notably *An American Imperative* (1993), which advocated for putting student learning first; ACPA's *Student Learning Imperative* (1996); AAHE, ACPA, and NASPA's *Powerful Partnerships* (1998); the National Association of State Universities and Land Grant Colleges (NASULGC)'s *Returning to Our Roots: The Student Experience* (1997); AAHE's promotion of such powerful pedagogies as service learning and their assessment forums; and the Association of American Colleges and Universities (AAC&U)'s *Greater Expectations* (2002), to name a few, all focused on the student as learner and identified partnerships across the institutional environment to promote learning and development.

Community colleges embraced this learning mission by identifying learning-centered colleges nationally and advancing a student-centered model through the Vanguard Colleges. NASPA and ACPA's *Learning Reconsidered* (2004) built on the visionary thinking of these, and other previous reports, to advance the dual message that academic learning and personal development are intertwined, reciprocal processes that could just be called learning, and indeed, that learning is inherently developmental and personal. In addition, *Learning Reconsidered* admonished institutions to identify the learning outcomes they seek to promote and identify how all resources of the environment (including the co-curriculum) affect those outcomes.

3. **Accountability.** State legislatures began asking similar questions of higher education

that they had posed to the K-12 sector. Just as the 2001 No Child Left Behind Act led to standards of learning in the K-12 sector, external stakeholders examining higher education, including regional accreditation bodies, sought to hold higher education institutions accountable for their asserted outcomes. Legislatures initiated mandatory accountability measures, such as demonstrating outcomes before reauthorizing select funding, and in some cases holding community colleges accountable for the success rates of their students when they transferred to four-year institutions.

Fueled by the *U.S. News & World Report* rankings frenzy, public accountability now includes students and their parents comparing institutions with data findings seeking assurance that they will get what they seek. Now, the Secretary of Education, Margaret Spellings, has appointed a Commission on Higher Education that is focused on demands for greater accountability.

4. **Assessment.** After years of advocating assessment as an institutional practice, higher education institutions had, by the mid-1990s, provided evidence only of student satisfaction, at best, and examples of broad-based evidence of accomplishing student outcomes were rare; Alverno College was praised as one of the most comprehensive models.

A new emphasis on assessment from many stakeholders has grown exponentially. The range of national assessment tools, including the venerable Cooperative Institutional Research Program (CIRP; an assessment of entering students) and College Student Experience Questionnaire (CSEQs), expanded with the addition of surveys by Noel-Levitz and a number of new measures, including the National

Survey of Student Engagement (NSSE). Building on the pre-1990's studies that examined what colleges actually do that engages students (i.e., *Involving Colleges*, 1991), recent books document a breadth of research on the student experience, and, specifically, how the college experience influences student outcomes. See *Promoting Reasonable Expectations: Aligning Student and Institutional Views of the College Experience* (Miller, Bender, & Schuh, 2005), *Student Success in College: Creating Conditions that Matter* (Kuh, Kinzie, Schuh, & Whitt, 2005) and the long awaited, *How College Affects Students: A Third Decade of Research* (Pascarella & Terenzini, 2005).

5. **Accreditation.** Disciplinary-based accrediting associations have advanced standards and specific learning outcomes for many years for specific college programs such as academic majors. Regional accrediting organizations that accredit entire institutions have moved recently toward requiring all parts of the institution to identify their outcomes and provide evidence that they are accomplishing those outcomes for all students. The Council of Regional Accrediting Commissions (2003) noted:

> *As college costs have skyrocketed, and demands for nearly-universal student access to higher education have become more pronounced, the questions asked of colleges by consumers and lawmakers have become more strident: "What are students learning? Is it the right kind of learning? What difference are you making in their lives? What evidence do you have that you're worth our investment?" (www.msache.org/msache/content/ pdf_files/Regnlsl.pdf)*

In their *Principles for Good Practices,* prepared for and endorsed by the Council of Regional Accrediting Commissions in 2003, the Council asked what an accrediting commission should reasonably expect of an institution, and, concerning the compilation of evidence of outcomes asserted:

> *Evidence of student learning is derived from multiple sources, such as courses, curricula, and co-curricular programming, and includes effects of both intentional and unintentional learning experiences. Evidence collected from these sources is complementary and portrays the impact on the student of the institution as a whole. (www.msache.org/msache/content/ pdf_files/Regnlsl.pdf)*

The progress of activity in these five interconnected themes has led to a widely embraced orientation that institutions should identify specific outcomes they seek to develop in students and assess their effectiveness in developing those outcomes. Institutions, however, have not been adept at identifying what those outcomes are.

STUDENT OUTCOMES

From the early colonial days of educating young male students to be "gentleman scholars," many college outcomes have been general and vaguely understood. In the early 2000s, a number of publications proposed student outcomes to shape a comprehensive look at the college experience. Current taxonomies outline a range of outcomes that might vary in emphasis by institutional type.

In 2002, Hamrick, Evans, and Schuh synthesized outcomes research and identified five clusters of outcomes that society and students should expect from the college experience. They assert that college graduates should be:

1. **Educated Persons** who support lifetime learning, the importance of education to

one's life, and mastering bodies of knowledge that bring insight to oneself and one's world;

2. **Skilled Workers**—which emphasizes the career and workforce preparation role for colleges to help students identify their options and learn successful work related skills;

3. **Democratic Citizens,** a goal that affirms the role of civic engagement in public life and the contributions needed to further society;

4. **Self-aware and Interpersonally Sensitive Individuals,** who are needed to interact in today's diverse society, recognizing that personal identity and culture affect everything someone does in relation to others; and

5. **Life Skills Managers** able to construct and manage functions that promote their quality of life.

In the same year, a National Panel convened by AAC&U published *Greater Expectations: A New Vision for Learning as a Nation Goes to College.* This report advocated for transformative education that would truly educate and profoundly change students as they experience any college environment. This panel encouraged campuses to develop students to be "empowered through the mastery of intellectual and practical skills, informed by knowledge about the natural and social worlds and about forms of inquiry basic to these studies, and responsible for their personal actions and for civic values." Specifically, they encourage all kinds and types of campuses to work with students through "practical liberal education" to produce those three major outcomes.

Recognizing that standards of practice were not complete without addressing the student outcomes to which they were directed, in 2003, the Council for the Advancement of Standards in Higher Education (CAS) incorporated 16 individual outcomes into each of their functional area standards (which now number more than 30). Not clustered in any schema, these outcomes were: intellectual growth, effective communication, enhanced self-esteem, realistic self-appraisal, clarified values, career choices, leadership development, healthy behavior, meaningful interpersonal relationships, independence, collaboration, social responsibility, satisfying and productive lifestyles, appreciating diversity, spiritual awareness, and personal and educational goals. CAS will publish *Frameworks for the Assessment of Learning and Development Outcomes* (FALDOs) in 2006.

Concurrent with all of this activity involving outcomes, NASPA and ACPA in 2002 convened a panel that developed *Learning Reconsidered.* This panel reviewed existing research on college outcomes and the recently emergent taxonomies and proposed a set of seven clusters that incorporated the breadth of scholarship on student outcomes. These outcomes were described in brief and examples of learning experiences across the campus where they might develop were identified. Further, the document identified examples of theoretical and conceptual frames that would assist educators in developing those outcomes.

KEY CONSIDERATIONS

There are several key considerations in identifying student outcomes for a particular program, function, or entire campus. These questions may help users identify key issues in articulating specific outcomes for a specific entity.

- **Mission, mission, mission.** What is the mission of the department, division, college or university? What different emphasis on any particular outcome cluster might be appropriate at a Jesuit institution or a land grant institution or a community college or a research university?

How might the outcome constellation be different for a health center whose mission is to treat student illness from a health center whose mission is to develop healthy lifestyles and wellness awareness in all students? Essentially, what is it that you want students to learn that will move them closer to achieving the mission of the program, division, or college?

Greater Expectations: Desired Student Outcomes

The empowered learner. The intellectual and practical skills that students need are extensive, sophisticated, and expanding with the explosion of new technologies. As they progress through grades K-12 and the undergraduate years, and at successively more challenging levels, students should learn to:

- effectively communicate orally, visually, in writing, and in a second language
- understand and employ quantitative and qualitative analysis to solve problems
- interpret and evaluate information from a variety of sources
- understand and work within complex systems and with diverse groups
- demonstrate intellectual agility and the ability to manage change
- transform information into knowledge and knowledge into judgment and action.

The informed learner. While intellectual and practical skills are essential, so is a deeper understanding of the world students inherit, as human beings and as contributing citizens. This knowledge extends beyond core concepts to include ways of investigating human society and the natural world. Both in school and college, students should have sustained opportunities to learn about:

- the human imagination, expression, and the products of many cultures
- the interrelations within and among global and cross-cultural communities
- means of modeling the natural, social, and technical worlds
- the values and histories underlying U.S. democracy.

The responsible learner. The integrity of a democratic society depends on citizens' sense of social responsibility and ethical judgment. To develop these qualities, education should foster:

- intellectual honesty
- responsibility for society's moral health and for social justice
- active participation as a citizen of a diverse democracy
- discernment of the ethical consequences of decisions and actions
- deep understanding of one's self and respect for the complex identities of others, their histories, and their cultures.

Source: Greater Expectations National Panel (2002).

Table I
Student Learning Outcomes*

Learning Reconsidered, 2004

Student Outcomes*	Dimensions of Outcomes	Sample Developmental Experiences for Learning	Bodies of Knowledge for Educators	Sample Learning Outcomes
Cognitive complexity	Critical thinking, reflective thinking, effective reasoning, intellectual flexibility, emotion/cognition integration, identity/cognition integration	Classroom teaching, readings and discussions; campus speakers; problem based learning; action research; study abroad; learning communities; living-learning communities; campus newspaper and media; cultural advocacy groups; LGBT awareness programs; diversity programs; group work in diverse teams; judicial board involvement	Cognitive development, identity development, interpersonal sensitivity, neurolinguistics, epistemology, reflective judgment, orders of consciousness, pedagogy	Students will be able to articulate the pro's and con's about a complex issue and formulate their own position regarding that issue.
Knowledge acquisition, integration, and application	Understanding knowledge from a range of disciplines (acquisition); connecting knowledge to other knowledge, ideas, and experiences (integration); relate knowledge to daily life (application); pursuit of lifelong learning; career decidedness; technological competence	Majors, minors, general education requirements, certificate programs; laboratories; action research; research teams; service learning; group projects; internships; jobs (on/ off campus); career development courses and programs; living-learning communities; Web-based information search skills; activities programming boards (e.g. film, concerts); drama, arts, and music groups; literary magazines; special teams and activities (e.g. solar car, Model UN)	Experiential learning, Cognitive development, identity development, interpersonal sensitivity, neurolinguistics, epistemology, learning theory; career development	Students will be able to relate how what they are learning connects to their current and future life experiences.

Table I — (continued)

Student Outcomes*	Dimensions of Outcomes	Sample Developmental Experiences for Learning	Bodies of Knowledge for Educators	Sample Learning Outcomes
Humanitari-anism	understanding and appreciation of human differences; cultural competency; social responsibility	diverse membership of student organizations; inter-group dialogue programs; service learning; community-based learning; cultural festivals; identity group programming (e.g. LGBT); ally programs; programs on world religions; study abroad; interdisciplinary courses; curriculum transformation	Racial identity development, multi-cultural competence, sexual/gender identity development; campus climate; reflective judgment, orders of consciousness, moral development, cognitive development	Students will be able to describe their own cultural identity, as well as analyze how that impacts their experience in the larger community.
Civic Engagement	sense of civic responsi-bility; commitment to public life through communities of practice; engage in principled dissent; effective in leadership	Involvement in student organizations; service learning; various student governance groups like student government/ resident hall government/ commuter student association; sports teams; community based organizations (e.g. PTA, neighborhood coalitions); emerging leader programs; leadership courses; open forums; teach-ins; activism and protest; community standards codes; student judicial boards; involvement in academic department/ major; identity with campus community	Leadership theory, socio-political theory, community development, group dynamics, organizational development and change theory, moral development, orders of consciousness	Students will recognize opportunities for making responsible, reflective decisions about and for both themselves and the community around them.

Table I — (continued)
Student Learning Outcomes*

Learning Reconsidered, 2004

Student Outcomes*	Dimensions of Outcomes	Sample Developmental Experiences for Learning	Bodies of Knowledge for Educators	Sample Learning Outcomes
Interpersonal and intrapersonal competence	Realistic self appraisal and self understanding; personal attributes such as identity, self esteem, confidence, ethics and integrity, spiritual awareness, personal goal setting; meaningful relationships; interdependence; collaboration; ability to work with people different from self	Identity based affinity groups; personal counseling; academic/life planning; roommate dialogues; individual advising; support groups; peer mentor programs; religious life programs and youth groups; student led judicial boards; paraprofessional roles (e.g. resident assistants, peer tutors, sexual assault advisors, peer mentor programs); disability support services; student employment; classroom project groups; classroom discussions	Psychosocial theory; identity development; interpersonal sensitivity; multiple intelligences; spiritual development, moral and ethical development	Students will identify behaviors of healthy relationships and design ways in which they will engage in healthy relationships with others. Students will be willing to take initial steps to resolving conflicts without seeking outside assistance. Students will be able to describe their skills and interests and make appropriate choices of major and early career steps.

Table I — (continued)

Student Outcomes*	Dimensions of Outcomes	Sample Developmental Experiences for Learning	Bodies of Knowledge for Educators	Sample Learning Outcomes
Practical competence	Effective communication; capacity to manage one's personal affairs; economic self-sufficiency and vocational competence; maintain personal health and wellness; prioritize leisure pursuits; living a purposeful and satisfying life	Campus recreation programs; food service and health center programs; drug and alcohol education; career development courses and programs; financial planning programs; club sports and recreation programs; senior council transition programs; personal counseling; academic/personal advising; portfolios; senior capstone course	Psychosocial theory; self-efficacy; career development; spiritual development; self-authorship	Students will formulate an intentional curricular and co-curricular plan for their collegiate journey.
Persistence and academic achievement	Manage the college experience to achieve academic and personal success; leading to academic goal success including degree attainment	Learning skills; bridge programs; peer mentoring; faculty and staff mentoring; supplemental instruction-tutoring; orientation programs; academic advising; financial aid; disability support services; parents' programs; child care services	Retention theory, person-environment fit, socialization, family systems	Students will make a schedule for completion of degree and be able to follow or revise it as necessary. Students will learn to use campus resources to support their learning and personal needs.

Source: Adapted from *Learning Reconsidered.*

Note: Learning Reconsidered defines *learning* as a comprehensive, holistic, transformative activity that integrates *academic learning and student development*, processes that have often been considered separate, and even independent of each other.

- **The philosophy behind what outcomes are valued.** The identification of outcomes is often a political process based on profound philosophical differences among key constituencies of what the college should be doing, and what its values are. How do the philosophy and values of the institution shape the outcomes valued in that environment? Those who only value the college's responsibility to develop the mind often do not find it appropriate for the college to seek to develop practical or inter- or intra- personal outcomes. But even educators who define only the cognitive outcomes (e.g., critical thinking and knowledge acquisition) might realize that those are developed in a variety of campus environments, including, for example, classrooms, judicial boards, student leadership positions, and service. In Chapter 3, Borrego outlines the mapping of all kinds of learning experiences across campus.

- **Assessment.** How can the outcomes be measured? How are espoused outcomes different from those actually developed? True assessment would benefit from Astin's (2001) inputs-environment-outcomes (IEO) theoretical model (controlling for pre-college inputs) to truly measure the effect on the outcome and identify aspects of the college environment that predict that outcome. The IEO model is being widely used in assessment. But some outcomes may only manifest themselves with a delayed effect; for example, developing civic awareness in students may not be measurable as civic engagement unless assessed with a post-college study.

APPLICATIONS IN PRACTICE

The two primary approaches to outcomes in practice are (a) drawing the bulls-eye first, and then figuring out how to hit it; or (b) drawing a circle around the hole later. The first approach (outcome to practice) is to identify a student learning outcome and identify existing or new programs that might be needed to develop that outcome in targeted students. This approach is intentional and planned. The second approach (practice to outcome) is to take any existing program and map it onto the learning outcome clusters to see which ones it most likely advances. In either case, assessment data are needed to determine whether the intervention (e.g., program or policy) contributes to the development of that outcome.

- **Outcome to practice.** A residence life program seeking to advance the outcome cluster of humanitarianism illustrates the first approach. The residence life department might design floor programs that promote appreciation of cultural differences. Activities that could develop that outcome might include team-building activities at the start of the year, cultural programming, diverse music at floor events, inter-group dialogue programs, mentoring or support groups focused on racial and ethnic differences, policies that insist roommates address their conflicts (some of which may be based in different world views or cultural experiences) with mediated discussions before any room re-assignment is possible, etc.

- **Practice to outcome.** The second approach is to take an existing program, such as a resume workshop in the career center, and chart it onto the learning outcomes grid, demonstrating which outcomes are developed by that program. A resumé workshop might contribute to knowledge application, intrapersonal competence, and practical competence. Exhibit 1 illustrates this process using the example of the leadership programs at the University of Maryland, College Park. Mapping all the programs of a specific office, or division, or the whole college would illustrate where there are gaps in offerings and for which groups of students these might be differentially available.

However, it is important to note that in this second approach we are *not* advocating taking existing programs and forcing them to fit onto some learning outcomes grid based on what "sounds" good. Rather, if feedback has not been gathered about a program, it needs to be, and then, based on that feedback, a program can be mapped onto the grid. This may create opportunities for discussions about why certain programs exist and open doors for more creative, holistic ways of approaching some of the student learning outcomes; we encourage these discussions to take place. Regardless of the approach, assessment data are critical to know if those programs do accomplish the intended goals.

WRITING OUTCOMES

Outcomes usually identify growth in some dimension of knowing, being, or doing. This knowledge (cognitive), attitude (affective), and skill (psychomotor) schema identifies three key categories of possible outcomes. See http://www.nwlink.com/~donclark/hrd/bloom.html for a

Table 2
Cognitive Development Model

Competence	Example of skill	Cue works/action verbs
Knowledge	Knowledge of key ideas, events, dates, places, people, information; mastery of a subject; quoting facts and information	Tell, describe, name, quote, label, list, name, recognize
Comprehension	Understanding information; translate information into a new setting; interpret or contrast sets of information; predict implications	Interpret, describe, contrast, predict, differentiate
Application	Solve problems using acquired knowledge; apply methods or theories to new problems	Apply, solve, examine, relate, classify, discover, operate
Analysis	Observe patterns in information; reveal hidden meanings	Analyze, explain, compare, deconstruct, connect, infer, troubleshoot
Synthesis	Form hypotheses from facts; integrate knowledgefrom diverse sources; build a whole from various parts	Integrate, generalize, design, formulate, prepare, revise
Evaluation	Judge value of theories or information; support evidence; recognize bias and subjectivity	Assess, measure, summarize, conclude

Source: Adapted from Bloom (1956); Counselling Services/University of Victoria (http://www.coun.uvic.ca/learn/program/hndouts/bloom.html); D. Clark (1999; http://www.nwlink.com/~donclark/hrd/bloom.html).

presentation on all three growth domains. Most college educators have had little to no experience stating measurable outcomes. K-12 educators have long found basic resources like Bloom's taxonomy (1956) to be helpful in creating outcome language. Bloom's taxonomy categorizes levels of complexity assuming that lower levels are embedded in higher level processes. Table 2 illustrates the levels of cognitive development.

A principle advanced by *Learning Reconsidered* should be restated here: Learning is not merely academic or cognitive learning; it is a transformative process including affective development and identity. It would be a mistake to use only Bloom's cognitive structures in writing outcomes, but they do provide a useful illustration of the sequence of learning and action verbs that may be stated in measurable ways to develop learning outcomes.

Kegan and developing outcomes. Another tool that is useful for writing learning outcomes is Robert Kegan's (1982) theory of lifespan development. Kegan (1994) asserts that an evolutionary activity of a person's meaning-making system (how one makes sense of the world around them) is the foundation for identity, and defines this evolution around the cognitive (how one makes sense of knowledge), interpersonal (the way in which one sees oneself in relation to others), and intrapersonal (an internally generated belief system) dimensions of development within his theory. He offers the idea of a subject-object balance as the construct through which the dimensions of development are intertwined and grow toward greater complexity resulting in a more complex meaning-making system.

People are embedded in the world around them, and how we are embedded is what "leads us to project into the world our construction of reality" (Kegan, 1982, p. 31), and it is also the specifics of how we are embedded that identify our current subject-object balance. It is when the specific way that we are embedded moves from subject to object that we emerge from our embeddedness and upon reintegration move what was subject to object, and

therefore further define our own unique internal meaning-making system (lifelong learning has occurred). It is also when our surroundings challenge us to emerge from our embeddedness, and we do not have the proper support structures around us, that we have the potential to feel crisis or the need to remove ourselves from our surroundings. At the same time, when our surroundings challenge us to emerge from our embeddedness, and we have the proper support structures, we move toward developing, "an internal compass to achieve complex learning" (Baxter Magolda, 2003, p. 232). Therefore, because complex learning is a goal of higher education it is important to create learning outcomes that challenge students to emerge from their embeddedness by connecting to their cognitive, interpersonal, and intrapersonal dimensions of development.

Example of outcomes in practice. An example of outcomes created to connect to the cognitive, interpersonal, and intrapersonal dimensions of development within the same learning experience are the following taken from Florida State University:

- *Greek Leadership Summit*—a two-day program facilitated by the Office of Greek Life for fraternity/sorority executive boards. A group of outcomes could be written as follows.

  At the conclusion of the program, participants will be able to:

  - Identify expectations Greek leaders have for the Office of Greek Life *(interpersonal)*

  - Apply the Office of Greek Life's expectations to various aspects of their Greek leader experience *(intrapersonal)*

  - Identify chapter and/or Greek traditions that are (are not) beneficial to the organization and broader Greek community *(cognitive, interpersonal)*; and

- Identify ways councils and/or chapters can partner together to enhance positive components of the Greek experience *(interpersonal)*.

- *Ethics Course*—a program designed by the Office of Student Rights and Responsibilities as a sanction for those found responsible for violating a conduct regulation. A group of outcomes could be written as follows.

At the conclusion of the program, participants will:

- Have increased self-awareness of how their values and ethics affect their personal decision making *(intrapersonal)*;

- Have increased awareness and concern for how their decisions affect the FSU community *(interpersonal)*;

- Understand why Florida State University believes it is important for them to consider the outcomes of their choices before acting upon them and will be motivated to improve in this area *(cognitive)*.

- Be able to recognize the differences between ethical and unethical choices in case studies.

- Be able to create ethical responses to typical situations in student life that tend to result in disciplinary action (e.g., underage drinking, use of previously published material in papers without citations, vandalism, etc.)

Experiential learning. Using Baxter Magolda's Principles of Learning (2003), Kolb's experiential learning cycle (see: http://www.learningandteaching.info/learning/experience.htm) is helpful in creating learning outcomes, experiences, and assessment tools. Other sources such as Bloom's taxonomy

(http://www.coun.uvic.ca/learn/program/hndouts/bloom.html) and the CAS standards (2003) are also helpful in developing learning outcomes.

Baxter Magolda's studies of college student learning led her to identify three key principles that promote transformative learning and self-authorship. Baxter Magolda's principles are:

1. Validating the learner as knower,

2. Situating the learning in the learner's experience, and

3. Co-creating the learning with the learner.

Kolb's experiential learning cycle consists of four stages, all of which flow from each other:

1. Concrete experience,

2. Reflective observation,

3. Abstract conceptualization, and

4. Active experimentation.

It is helpful to examine two examples of writing measurable learning outcomes using these principles, one from an introductory core course and the other related to advising a student organization. Assume that an institution, using one of the techniques discussed earlier, identifies cognitive complexity, knowledge acquisition, integration, and application, as well as persistence and academic achievement as student outcomes that would achieve the mission of the institution. You are then expected to take those outcomes and work toward them in the introductory core course that you are teaching. Rather than start with the experience, as many do on Kolb's experiential learning cycle, by being given student outcomes you start with abstract conceptualization. What is it that you want students to learn from your course? Often professors answer this question in the course expectations section of the syllabus and share with students what they can expect to "take away" from the course.

Then you move into the active experimentation and concrete experimentation stages of Kolb's cycle. It is important to remember that Kolb's cycle is fluid, especially within the context of a classroom where meaning-making is mutually constructed. This is where Baxter Magolda's Principles of Learning can assist in creating a learning environment. By applying Baxter Magolda's Principles, the learning outcomes identified for the core course are transformed into an experience in which academic learning and personal development occur—into a *learning environment*.

- *Course example.* A professor may identify a learning outcome to be that students will learn to identify the pros and cons of the introductory core course subject by the end of the course. This can be accomplished by asking students in the course to list all of the pros and cons that they can think of at the beginning of the course, which validates them by acknowledging that they already bring information with them to the learning environment. This list could then be revisited throughout the course, each time asking them to build on it.

  They may then be asked to come prepared to class ready to discuss the material with guidance/lecture from the instructor. Doing so not only continues to validate the student as a knower, but also co-creates the learning between the instructor and the students. In larger classes this may appear daunting; however, breaking a large classroom into small group discussions can be helpful, as well as forming one's lecture to help students as they think through the issues being presented for themselves [further examples can be found in *Creating Contexts* (Baxter Magolda, 1999)]. Finally, by encouraging students to create their own

list of pro's and con's and co-creating the learning that occurs with them the students' own experiences are being invited into the classroom.

During and at the conclusion of such an experience it is important for the professor to assess whether or not they have achieved their learning outcomes, illustrating Kolb's reflective observation stage. Assignments completed throughout the course of the semester can be used to evaluate where students are in terms of achieving the learning outcomes. It is important to structure the assignments/questions in a way that they get at the purpose of the learning outcomes. So instead of simply just asking the question of whether or not a student can list pro's and con's of the course material, it is important to ask why and how they learned the pro's and con's, as well as what they think of them. This insight can then guide the instructor in terms of shaping the environment to reach the learning outcomes, as well as plan for teaching a similar course in the future.

- *Advising a student group example.* A similar process occurs when one is creating learning outcomes for advising a student group such as the Interfraternity Council (IFC), a governing body for fraternities. The student outcomes identified for the department that oversees advising such a group may be humanitarianism, civic engagement, and interpersonal and intrapersonal competence. Again, if one starts with the abstract conceptualization stage of Kolb's experiential learning theory, then one would look at the purpose of the IFC and come up with a list of responses to the question: What do we want to "get out of" (learn from) this experience of being on IFC?

  Just by answering this question and using Baxter Magolda's principles moves us into the active experimentation and concrete experimentation stages of Kolb's learning cycle. For example, by holding a retreat at the beginning of the school year in which the students are asked to identify what they hope others will learn from their experience with IFC validates them as knowers by acknowledging that as members of the Greek community they bring important knowledge to the table. It also allows them the opportunity to situate the learning in their experience, and, through the guidelines of what a student organization can and cannot do according to institutional policy and federal and state law (as well as the mission of the organization), the learning that occurs is co-created (notice this is not a free-for-all). Then, throughout the year and before the conclusion of the year, it is important to assess how well they are working toward achieving those learning outcomes (Kolb's reflective observation stage). Assessment such as taking intentional time out of the meeting to revisit the goals for the year and reflecting on them, asking those groups which the IFC governs for their feedback, and spending one-on-one time with each IFC member in which they are asked specifically how they are personally helping the IFC reach its goals are just a few ways of assessing such outcomes. Then, after each of these experiences, it is important to follow up with written documentation as to what was learned from these assessments. These data can then be used to set goals for the following year.

METHODS, TECHNIQUES, AND ACTIVITIES

A variety of methods might be used to identify learning outcomes and prioritize the degree of emphasis to be placed on them. An entire campus or each internal entity (e.g., a functional area, a major) should begin by identifying the learning outcomes it seeks to develop in its students. A variety of methods might help engage stakeholders in those discussions.

- **Outcomes sort.** Create a separate card or slip of paper for each specific outcome a college, division, or function could realistically influence. State the outcome and include a brief definition of what that outcome might include. Give a set of cards to individuals and ask them to rank order them from most to least important for that context. Engage in small group discussions building to larger group discussion. An alternate approach is to give a handout with a list of outcomes and ask them to be ranked "essential," "desirable," or "optional." Discussion should include the label and outcome definitions used to open dialogue on intended meanings.

- **Ideal graduate (or participant, or new professional).** Give everyone a pad of yellow sticky notes. Using a felt marker, ask them to write a word or phrase to identify something they would hope an ideal program participant or college graduate would be able to know, be or do as a result of engaging with your program or college. What is it that an ideal program participant would learn from the experience? Brainstorm as many as individuals can identify. In teams of five or six people, put all the sticky notes on a wall surface and cluster them into categories. Build your own learning outcome goal clusters through these themes. An alternative is to select three or four from any one theme and state them as measurable learning outcomes. A subsequent mapping activity could identify where those outcomes are now developed across the environment (see Chapter 3). Exhibit 2 is a list of learning outcomes identified by the Reid Campus Center staff at Whitman College.

- **Stakeholders ratings.** After identifying any list of outcomes appropriate to the context, design a web survey asking stakeholder groups (e.g., new students, graduating seniors, faculty, student development educators, alumni, parents) to rank each outcome based on its importance to learning at this institution and on how well the institution provides an opportunity for that learning. Similar to the Institutional Goals Inventory (IGI) or Institutional Functioning Inventory (IFI), this allows for patterns of difference to emerge. A more complex assessment could also ask where these learning opportunities are occurring. This kind of information helps to allocate resources responsibly and identifies environmental factors that influence learning so staff can explore what makes those experiences so powerful.

- **Accreditation outcomes review.** Assemble the standards statements for all the programs on campus that must be accredited to continue. Do a content analysis of those outcomes and look for themes. Map the institutional environment to see how those themes are addressed. Sample Web pages of disciplinary outcomes statements appear in Appendix A.

These examples illustrate how educators may create learning outcomes, environments, and assessment tools in their role. It is important not only to make sure that educators create measurable learning outcomes for their situation, but also that they formulate and utilize assessment tools that evaluate the learning that is occurring. Baxter Magolda's MER, Love and Estenak's (2004) *Rethinking Student Affairs Practice,* the National Survey of Student Engagement (NSSE), and an institution's department of institutional research are all helpful resources for creating these materials.

Exhibit 1
The Maryland Leadership Outcomes Project

[Chapter authors' note: The leadership team at Maryland (a group of professional leadership educators in the office of campus programs) developed this use of Learning Reconsidered; they identified 22 learning outcomes using the framework of the Learning Reconsidered categories and then mapped the work of their various offices against that grid. They are now reviewing what gaps and strengths they have. This is reprinted with their permission.]

Towards a UM Leadership Center:
How an Integrated Approach Promotes Student Learning Outcomes

In 2004, ACPA and NASPA came together to produce *Learning Reconsidered*, a powerful document that argues for the integrated use of all of higher education's resources in the education and preparation of the whole student. This document introduces new ways of understanding and supporting learning and development as intertwined, inseparable elements of the student experience. It advocates for transformative education—a holistic process of learning that places the student at

(continued on next page)

the center of the learning experience (Purpose Statement, *Learning Reconsidered*, 2004). The transformative nature of the document acknowledges the role student affairs plays in connecting learning across the broader campus and community, and calls for a collaborative, systemic approach to promoting student learning.

The Maryland Leadership Development Program (MLDP) at the University of Maryland College Park used the *Learning Reconsidered* document as a springboard for clarifying and developing our own set of intended learning outcomes for students participating in our curricular and co-curricular programs. We identified 22 core learning outcomes, clustered into 6 broader categories, related to leadership development and student involvement (see attached matrix and key). Coordinators will develop and adapt existing leadership programs to intentionally promote any combination of these outcomes. These outcomes will also be assessed annually so that student progress toward learning can be measured. It is our hope to use these assessment results for program improvement and refinement, as well as to be able to effectively communicate to students the benefits of involvement at Maryland. An additional benefit of clearly stated and regularly assessed learning outcomes is our ability to benchmark our leadership and involvement programs against other campus offerings as well as institutional peers.

The process of identifying core learning outcomes related to leadership and involvement proffered interesting insights. First, the MLDP staff realized the intertwined and multi-dimensional nature of our programmatic offerings. No one program or service adequately promoted all 22 learning outcomes. While some programs offered a broad spectrum of learning opportunities, others had more defined, specific goals. We realized the importance of intentionally communicating intended outcomes to students in advance of their participation in our programs and services. This also means reviewing programs to be sure they are serving students to the best extent possible. Secondly, the process of reviewing our programs and services led us to identify possible areas of collaboration across units of the Lead Team, and the campus at large. For example, we decided that co-curricular leadership programming could be more intentional about targeting leadership development opportunities for non-positional leaders in all student organizations, including groups sponsored by Residence Life and other campus departments. Another area of interest was the potential overlap in administering leadership curricular offerings and curricular service-learning courses.

It was insights such as these that demonstrated both the need for, and potential benefits of, a more integrated approach to student leadership and involvement opportunities at Maryland. Coordinating programs and services across functional units, with an eye toward promoting a broad spectrum of student learning outcomes, would allow us to continue these discussions of what is the best way to put the holistic learning and development of students first, and not be hemmed by traditional functional lines, or "we've always done it that way" thinking. More centralized resources and advising, coupled with the resulting increased visibility of our programs to student and campus communities, would allow us to shape an intentional campus culture of leadership and involvement. We would be capitalizing on Maryland's national reputation for leadership, and re-organizing units in a way that will allow us to go, in Jim Collins' words, "from good to great". Following (University of Maryland, College Park President) Mote's President's Promise Initiative, a more integrated, multi-faceted, intentional approach to student involvement and leadership would allow us to more effectively offer those promised "opportunities for leadership that only a university adjacent to the nation's capital can provide."

Maryland Leadership Development Program (MLDP)
Intended Learning Outcomes By Program
University of Maryland 2004-05

Intended Learning Outcomes	COGNITIVE COMPLEXITY				KNOWLEDGE ACQUISITION, INTEGRATION, & APPLICATION						HUMANI-TARIANISM			CIVIC ENGAGEMENT			INTER-PERSONAL & INTRA-PERSONAL			PRACTICAL COMPETENCE		
	1	2	3	4	5	6	7	8	9	10	11	12	13	14	15	16	17	18	19	20	21	22
MLDP Programs	X	X		X																		
Student Organizations and GSG																						
General Organization Support		X	X	X					X						X		X		X	X	X	X
SGA Funding Process Advising	X	X		X	X				X					X	X		X		X	X	X	X
SGA Finance Committee Advising	X	X		X	X		X		X		X	X		X	X		X		X	X	X	X
Student Fiduciary Training		X			X				X		X			X	X			X	X		X	X
Organization Advisor Training	X	X	X	X	X	X	X		X		X			X	X		X		X		X	X
Account Management				X					X											X	X	X
GSG Advising	X	X	X	X	X	X	X		X		X	X		X	X		X		X	X	X	X
Graduate Organization Support	X	X							X					X	X			X	X		X	X
GSG Funding Process Advising	X	X		X			X		X		X	X		X	X		X		X	X	X	X
Graduate Community Programming		X					X				X	X			X		X		X			X
Student Office Staff Management	X	X		X																	X	
Event Policy Planning Training																	X		X		X	X
Graduate Student Advocacy		X							X		X						X		X		X	X
Graduate Student Needs Assessment																						X
Customer Service Assessment												X									X	X
STAR Center Financial Support																					X	X
STARS System									X											X	X	X

Intended Learning Outcomes	COGNITIVE COMPLEXITY				KNOWLEDGE ACQUISITION, INTEGRATION, & APPLICATION						HUMANI-TARIANISM			CIVIC ENGAGEMENT			INTER-PERSONAL & INTRA-PERSONAL			PRACTICAL COMPETENCE		
	1	2	3	4	5	6	7	8	9	10	11	12	13	14	15	16	17	18	19	20	21	22
MLDP Programs	X																					
Co-Curricular Leadership Programs			X														X	X	X	X	X	X
Terrapin Leadership Institute (TLI)—Gateway			X														X	X	X	X	X	X
TLI—Group			X					X									X	X	X	X	X	X
TLI—Society			X				X				X		X	X		X	X	X	X			
Maryland Leadership Conference	X			X								X		X			X	X	X		X	
Emerging Leaders Conference			X														X	X	X		X	
M Class	X		X	X			X		X		X	X	X	X		X	X	X	X	X	X	X
Peer Leadership Council	X		X				X	X				X	X	X	X	X	X	X	X	X	X	X
Maryland Leadership Collaborative	X		X	X				X				X	X		X	X	X	X		X		X
Year-End Programs																X				X		
EDCP 317 Intro to Leadership	X	X	X	X	X		X	X	X	X	X	X	X	X	X	X	X	X	X	X	X	X
EDCP 318 Service & Leadership	X	X	X	X	X		X	X	X	X	X	X	X	X	X	X	X	X	X	X	X	X
EDCP 318 Orgs/President Class	X	X	X	X	X		X	X	X	X	X	X	X	X	X	X	X	X	X	X	X	X
EDCP 417 Advanced Leadership	X	X	X	X	X	X	X		X	X	X	X	X	X	X	X	X	X	X	X	X	X
EDCP 418 Identities & Leadership	X	X	X	X	X	X	X		X	X	X	X	X	X	X	X	X	X	X	X	X	X
EDCP 418 Diversity & Leadership	X	X	X	X	X	X	X		X	X	X	X	X	X	X	X	X	X	X	X	X	X

Maryland Leadership Development Program (MLDP)
Intended Learning Outcomes By Program
University of Maryland 2004-05

Intended Learning Outcomes	COGNITIVE COMPLEXITY					KNOWLEDGE ACQUISITION, INTEGRATION, & APPLICATION					HUMANI-TARIANISM			CIVIC ENGAGEMENT			INTER-PERSONAL & INTRA-PERSONAL			PRACTICAL COMPETENCE		
	1	2	3	4	5	6	7	8	9	10	11	12	13	14	15	16	17	18	19	20	21	22
MLDP Programs	X		X	X	X						X	X	X	X	X		X	X	X	X	X	X
CRC Adventure Challenge Course	X	X	X	X	X				X		X	X	X	X	X		X	X	X	X	X	X
Curricular Group Projects	X		X	X	X			X	X		X	X	X		X		X	X	X	X	X	X
Curricular Service-Learning	X		X	X	X		X	X	X	X	X	X	X	X	X	X	X	X	X	X	X	X
Myers-Briggs Type Indicator	X		X	X		X			X			X	X				X			X		
Exploring Leadership Textbook	X	X	X	X	X	X	X	X	X	X	X	X	X	X	X	X	X	X	X		X	X

Source: Maryland Leadership Development Program, University of Maryland, College Park (2004).

Learning Outcomes Key

Categories of learning outcomes drawn from *Learning Reconsidered*

COGNITIVE COMPLEXITY

Students will learn to . . .

1 = Engage with others in constructive ways Engage in principled dissent; accept and appreciate other worldviews; manage conflict constructively

2 = Develop critical thinking skills

3 = View leadership as a process, not a position

4 = Be open to change

KNOWLEDGE ACQUISITION, INTEGRATION, & APPLICATION

Students will learn to...

5 = Understand history of leadership and current leadership theories

6 = Understand identity development models

7 = Gain knowledge of diverse cultures and oppressed groups

8 = Value the multidisciplinarity of leadership Understand roots of leadership studies; integrate leadership learning across disciplines; enact leadership in specific contexts

9 = Practice systems thinking Understand group dynamics; understand organizational structures and political systems; navigate complex systems

10 = Be committed to life-long learning

HUMANITARIANISM

Students will learn to . . .

11 = Gain knowledge of humanitarian issues Understand uses of power and nature of oppression; be aware of cultural and personal differences

12 = Practice humanitarian skills Trust and respect others; empathize; access culturally appropriate resources

13 = Value humanitarian states of mind Be committed to cross-cultural communication; value social responsibility; be committed to social justice

CIVIC ENGAGEMENT

Students will learn to . . .

14 = Create effective change Practice collective efficacy

15 = Develop common purpose

16 = Develop civic awareness Value civic responsibility; practice engaged citizenship

INTERPERSONAL & INTRAPERSONAL COMPETENCE

Students will learn to . . .

17 = Gain knowledge about themselves Develop consciousness of self; self-confidence; feelings of mattering;

manage personal emotions; value cultural heritage

18 = Apply self-knowledge Practice self-efficacy; congruence; commitment; identify passions; discuss cultural differences and issues

19 = Work with others Practice collaboration; controversy with civility; engage across difference; be committed to ethical action

PRACTICAL COMPETENCE

Students will learn to . . .

20 = Develop effective communication skills Practice effective written and oral communication

21 = Develop personal leadership skills Set individual goals; practice risk-taking; delegate; serve as a role model; manage people and tasks; facilitate group processes

22 = Develop group leadership skills Develop leadership in peers; identify common purpose in groups; help groups set goals; apply problem solving strategies; value recognition and organizational sustainability

Source: Maryland Leadership Development Program, University of Maryland, College Park (2004).

Exhibit 2
General Learning Outcomes for
Students in Reid Campus Center Programs
Whitman College

- Leadership—Manage a program from start to finish.

- Critical Thinking Skills—Gather and organize information relevant to the subject under study, analyze the information and arguments, develop hypotheses, and construct convincing arguments or strategies.

- Organization/Planning Skills—Develop informal and formal statements of purpose, plan potential uses of resources, identify the criteria for success in achieving goals; systematize and arrange data pertinent to your goal.

- Implementation—Plan the steps and time frame needed to accomplish a task; select and organize appropriate resources and delegate tasks; manage the resources at the time and place of delivery.

- Reflection—Throughout the construction and implementation of strategies, assess where you are, where you're going, and where you would like to be.

- Decision-Making Skills—To be appropriate, objective and logical in making judgments and take responsibility for decisions.

- Initiative—Recognize an uncompleted task or potential opportunity or problem and do the job without being told; be a self-starter.

- Adaptability—Accept and meet others where they are; relate to many types of people and situations, and make transitions fluidly; be flexible.

- Problem Solving—Evaluate, assess, diagnose, generate alternatives, and anticipate needs.

- Communication Skills—Express oneself in a variety of ways with clarity and effectiveness.

- Relationship Building—Initiate, cultivate, and maintain professional contacts and interdepartmental partnerships.

- Team Work—Work collaboratively toward a common goal with others.

- Assertiveness—Speak for oneself in a clear, direct, and constructive manner.

- Financial Management Skills—Plan, develop, implement, monitor, and manage a budget.

- Comportment Skills—Present oneself in a manner appropriate for every circumstance.

- Confidentiality—Use discretion when dealing with liability, suitability, or any other delicate or high-risk matters.

- Safety—Apply and follow approved precautions and procedures at all times.

- Dress—Wear clothing that is suitable and appropriate for the population with which you are working and the job you will be doing.

- Speech—Use language that is suitable and appropriate for the populations with which you are working.

- Marketing—Create popular advertising mediums for your target audience.

- Recruit—Actively engage and incorporate interested participants into your programs.

- Customer Service—Assist your clientele quickly and pleasantly with any reasonable request they may present.

Source: Personal communication to Gregory Roberts, ACPA.

Exhibit 3
Writing Learning Outcomes
American University

Phase 1: Writing Learning Outcomes

- Try using this template for writing learning outcomes

As a result of students participating in _____   _____ ,

they will learn _____ .

Ex: *As a result of students participating in* the resident assistant (RA) training session for writing
IRF's (Incident Report Forms), *they will learn* to write concisely, include factual details in their
reports, and use language that is non-judgmental.

[The objectives of RA training are: knowledge acquisition, skill building, team building, and
task accomplishment.]

- After creating RA training learning outcomes, reference this checklist
  (adapted from "An Updated Criteria Checklist for an Assessment Program")

LEARNING OUTCOMES

1. Does the outcome support the program objectives?   Y   N

2. Does the outcome describe what the program intends for students to know
   (cognitive), think (affective, attitudinal), or do (behavioral, performance)?   Y   N

3. Is the outcome important/worthwhile?   Y   N

4. Is the outcome:

   a. Detailed and specific?   Y   N

   b. Measurable/identifiable?   Y   N

5. Can you create an activity to enable students to learn the desired outcome?   Y   N

6. Can the outcome be used to make decisions on how to improve the program?   Y   N

Source: Gail Short Hanson, American University.

Appendix A to Chapter 4
Sample Discipline Based Accreditation Standards/Learning Outcomes

See these sites for examples of how various disciplines approach outcomes in their fields. These reflect how learning outcomes are addressed in accreditation.

The Accreditation Board for Engineering and Technology
> http://clte.asu.edu/active/ABET%20Student%20Outcomes.pdf

Guidelines and Principles for Accreditation of Programs in Professional Psychology
Presents the 2000 version of the Guidelines and Principles for Accreditation of Programs in Professional Psychology.
> http://www.apa.org/ed/gp2000.html

What psych majors need to know
APA Monitor article (Jul-Aug 2002) describing a document endorsed by APA's Board of Educational Affairs that outlines the expectations and learning goals for the undergraduate psychology major.
> *http://www.apa.org/monitor/julaug02/psychmajors.html*

National Environmental Health Science and Protection Accreditation
> http://www.ehacoffice.org/process/ps_under.php

Council on Social Work Education (http://www.cswe.org/)
> http://www.cswe.org/accreditation/EPAS Revised 10-04.pdf
> Page 7: 3.0 Foundation Program Objectives

Agricultural Systems Technology, Iowa State University
> http://learn.ae.iastate.edu/assessment/snapshot.htm

See these sites for examples of how different divisions/departments within an institution approach fulfilling the mission of the institution.

Bridgewater State College—Student Learning Outcomes
> http://www.bridgew.edu/StudentAffairs/stulrnoutcm.pdf

California State University—Student Learning Outcomes
> http://www.calstate.edu/AcadAff/Sloa/links/student_affairs.shtml

Longwood University
> http://www.longwood.edu/studentaffairs/

Spokane Community College—Abilities of a Spokane Community College Student
>   http://www.scc.spokane.edu/assessment/

Texas Christian University
>   http://www.assessment.tcu.edu/assessment.html

University of Minnesota—Office of Student Affairs Student Success Outcomes
>   http://www.osa.umn.edu/outcomes/index.html

Wells College Mission and Institutional Goals 2002-2003 Catalog.

Westminster College Mission and Outcomes Statements
>   http://www.westminster.edu/acad/oaac/assess_mission.cfm

Websites with Kolb resources
>   http://www.infed.org/biblio/b-explrn.htm
>   http://reviewing.co.uk/research/experiential.learning.htm#26
>   http://reviewing.co.uk/research/learning.cycles.htm
>   http://www.learningandteaching.info/learning/experience.htm

Websites with Bloom resources
>   http://www.coun.uvic.ca/learn/program/hndouts/bloom.html
>   http://www.nwlink.com/~donclark/hrd/bloom.html
>   http://www.teachers.ash.org.au/researchskills/dalton.htm

CHAPTER 5
ASSESSING INTERNAL ENVIRONMENTS

Robert Bonfiglio
Gail Short Hanson
Jane Fried
Gregory Roberts
Jacqueline Skinner

"Assessment should be used as a feedback loop to tell students how they are doing and where they need to continue to improve."

Jane Fried

INTRODUCTION

A transition from a teaching-oriented to a student-centered learning environment requires institutional or divisional self-analysis or assessment; turning the results of that analysis into strategies; creating student learning experiences (that is, not just experiences unaligned with learning); and measuring the intended learning outcomes to determine whether the delivered experiences actually contribute to transformative learning in the context of institutional mission. All of these components are based on the answers to critical and sometimes tough questions that must be asked of your department, division and eventually the campus community during the transition process. What are those questions? And can simply asking critical questions be all that is really necessary to advance and guide the transition process? The obvious answer is no—but knowing what questions to ask sets the stage for change.

WHERE AND HOW TO BEGIN?

An increasingly rich literature now offers guidance as institutions begin or strengthen assessment efforts; comprehensive texts like Maki's *Assessing for Learning* (2004) offer both leadership and practical advice. A standard practice with which to begin assessments of programs and services within campus departments and divisions is to hold a staff retreat for one or more purposes: to help enhance professional skills, discuss cutting edge trends and their implications for work with students, review progress on the institutional or division strategic plan, or decide what new initiatives or strategies should be undertaken for the coming academic year. Retreats can provide a supportive context for discussion among staff members about the kinds of questions needed to inspire a focused and purposeful assessment process, and, because they generally center on longer term and strategic issues (rather than day-to-day tactics and problem solving), they can promote a richer conversation about divisional and institutional goals.

Some of the critical questions with which to begin framing an assessment process include these:

- Is the term "transformative learning" familiar at your institution? If so, how is it defined and used?

- Who is, or should be, responsible and accountable for identifying and articulating student learning outcomes in the context of transformative learning experience at your institution?

- What are the mutually agreed-upon characteristics of a transformative learning experience at your institution?

- How do you define the term "collaboration" as applied to work shared between faculty and student and campus life staff at your institution, and how is that collaboration manifested in the development and execution of transformative learning programs?

"Informative *learning changes what we know;* transformative *learning changes how we know." (Kegan, 2000, p. 50)*

Other questions help departments, divisions, and institutions ascertain ways to move from disparate learning experiences to a collaboration or partnership for learning. Expectations about integrating learning experiences may be explored with questions such as:

- Are the expected learning outcomes of both curricular and co-curricular programs at your institution identified and communicated regularly? Are they linked or unified?

- What are the expectations for faculty involvement in co-curricular programs at your institution? Are those expectations reasonable and attainable?

- What are the expectations for the participation of student affairs educators in curricular programs at your institution? Are those expectations reasonable and attainable?

- What are the expectations for student involvement in curricular and co-curricular programs at your institution? Are those expectations reasonable and attainable?

- Are there co-curricular experiences that every student is expected to engage in at your institution, such as a study abroad experience, volunteer service, an organizational leadership experience, a performance in the arts, or an internship? What areas of campus are involved in these experiences?

"*Learning is a complex, holistic, multicentric activity that occurs throughout and across the college experience"* (Learning Reconsidered, 2004, p.5).

The following suggested questions are designed to help an institution assess its culture and readiness for creating a student-learning environment.

- How is faculty participation in, and support of, co-curricular programs valued and rewarded at your institution?

- How is student involvement in co-curricular programs encouraged or impeded, and supported and rewarded at your institution?

- Does the quality and utility of the facilities at your institution represent the expectations of both the college/university and its students for transformative learning?

- Do administrative and organizational structures at your institution represent the expectations of both the college/university and its students for transformative learning?

- How does the demographic composition of the student body at your institution affect the goal of transformative student learning?

- Does the assessment of student learning follow published *Principles of Good Practice for Assessing Student Learning*? (Astin & Associates, 2003)

- Are ongoing professional development programs sponsored at your institution that address the concept of transformative learning?

FOCUSING ON STUDENT LEARNING OUTSIDE OF THE CLASSROOM: A CAMPUS EXAMPLE OF SUGGESTED FIRST STEPS FOR ASSESSING THE INTERNAL WORK ENVIRONMENT

One of the first projects that the division of student and campus life at SUNY-Geneseo began under the leadership of a new vice president was to conduct an analysis of the programs and services provided by the division by utilizing the Assessment Inventories based on the *Principles of Good Practices in Student Affairs* (1997) published by ACPA and NASPA. This assessment led the staff to conclude that the strengths of the division were as follows:

- Student affairs educators provide students with leadership training and offer leadership opportunities.

- Student affairs educators use a variety of communication methods to engage students' different learning styles.

- Students are informed that the institution has high expectation for their academic and personal achievements and active involvement in campus life.

- Students are encouraged to participate in activities that increase self-understanding and self-confidence.

- Programs are offered that address student needs for academic support, co-curricular involvement, and personal growth.

- The institution recognizes outstanding student accomplishments through rewards, honorary organizations, and other forms of public recognition.

- Student affairs educators participate in the development of programs that welcome new members of the community to the institution (e.g., new student orientation, transfer student orientation).

The assessment exercise revealed that some of the work of the division was already oriented toward student learning, especially leadership training and the development of self-understanding and self-confidence. It also identified a number of areas where the staff felt it was deficient and that needed improvement. Many staff members felt that some important principles of good practice did not characterize the student affairs program at their campus:

- Collaboration with faculty is promoted to integrate civic responsibility and service into the curriculum.

- Students are expected to understand and respect other students' experiences and perspectives.

- Faculty and students are included in developing the processes for adjudicating student misconduct.

- Student affairs educators are actively engaged in research to assess student learning outcomes.

- Research data is used to help student affairs educators understand what students are learning and to improve programs and services.

- Research priorities of the student affairs division are included in the institutional research agenda.

- Research results and their implications are communicated on a regular basis to faculty, staff, and students.

- Staff development programs are offered to assist staff in understanding and applying current research findings both on and off campus.

- Staff members are active in professional associations and present research findings both on and off campus.

- A strategic plan exists that links fiscal and human resources to desired educational outcomes.

- A systematic evaluation process is used to ensure that programs and services are cost effective.

- Student needs are assessed on a regular basis and resources are allocated accordingly.

- Resources are secured to incorporate new technologies into programs and activities.

- Educational outcomes are used to determine the design and use of indoor and outdoor learning spaces.

- Faculty and administrative staff from other divisions are routinely invited to student affairs staff meetings to discuss campus issues and program planning.

On other campuses, similar assessment discussions are generated by completing departmental self-assessment guides (SAGs) linked to the CAS Standards (Council for the Advancement of Standards in Higher Education, 2003). CAS, with representatives from more than 35 associations, has developed more than 30 standards that support assessments of the internal environment in student life programs and services; see www.cas.edu.

CREATING STRATEGIES, OBJECTIVES, AND GOALS

A common challenge for an institution, division, or department is to make good use of the assessment data collected for a particular purpose or project. Assessment data often remain in a summary report without further intentional attention; this is a waste of resources. Whatever assessment is undertaken to determine institutional readiness for transformative learning must be linked to action steps that can enhance strengths and address identified challenges.

Here is an example: Armed with the information garnered by asking the assessment questions described earlier, the vice president for student and campus life at SUNY-Geneseo charged the staff with the responsibility to create a series of key documents at divisional level, including vision and mission statements, goals, and learning outcomes that articulated the division's intent to place student learning at the center of its work. Once these major documents were drafted, critiqued, revised, and agreed upon by the staff, each department was asked to develop (or revise) its individual mission and goal statements, keeping in mind that each department's mission statement and goals had to flow from the division's mission statement and the broad goals previously developed.

- Mission statement: *The Division of Student and Campus Life has as its primary function the advancement of the mission of the College through the provision of a broad range of educational, social, and recreational programs, facilities, and fundamental services that foster the optimum living and learning environment on campus, facilitate the overall development of each student, and enhance the sense of community at the College.*

- Vision statement: *The Division of Student and Campus Life seeks to maximize the learning potential inherent in the programs and services it sponsors. As a learning-centered organization,*

- *Learning is our top priority.*

- *Learning is broadly defined.*

- *We have high expectations for learning.*

- *Learning is understood to be an active process based on the acceptance of responsibility to be both a learner and a teacher.*

- *Learning is understood to be an interactive process that takes place through community involvement with others regardless of title, role, or group affiliation, as all members of the community can be teachers and learners.*

- *Learning is understood to have a cumulative impact and is not merely a product to be consumed.*

- *Learning is understood to encompass the acquisition of knowledge and skills in the classroom, in structured co-curricular activities, and in informal interactions with others.*

- *Learning is facilitated by free and effective communication among all members of our community.*

- *Learning results from what we say and what we do as well as what we know, since teaching takes place through example.*

- *Learning is enriched by the diversity and inclusivity of the community.*

- *Learning is strengthened when what has been learned is applied to roles and situations that enable students to serve as ethical members of this and other communities.*

- *We aim to provide a foundation for a lifetime of learning.*

- **Goals:**

  - Students will assume responsibility for their own intellectual and social development.

  - Students will successfully complete the transition to college life.

  - Students will take full advantage of the opportunities both inside and outside of the classroom to learn from every member of the campus community.

  - Students will successfully prepare for post-graduate educational and occupational opportunities.

  - Students will become more fully self-aware.

  - Students will develop a personal values system consistent with the ideals of ethical citizenship.

  - Students will grow in their social and communication skills as evidenced by their ability to live and work collaboratively with others, engage in respectful relationships, and assume shared responsibility for the common good.

  - Students will develop leadership skills, and apply them in both the collegiate setting and in their communities upon graduation.

  - Students will develop an understanding of the global nature of our society and the interdependency of all people, and will demonstrate appreciation of the similarities and differences we all embody.

  - Students will develop habits consistent with a healthy lifestyle.

  - Students will develop an interest in and appreciation of the fine and performing arts.

  - The staff of the Division of Student and Campus Life will advocate for the rights and responsibilities of students.

ASSIGNING AND PERSONALIZING ROLES AND RESPONSIBILITIES

The authors of the *Student Learning Imperative* stated, "...if learning is the primary measure of institutional productivity by which the quality of undergraduate education is determined, what and how much students learn also must be the criterion by which the value of student affairs is judged" (American College Personnel Association, 1994, p. 2).

Because a focus on student learning requires that a staff be able to assess its impact on student learning, the staff was then directed to complete an inventory of ongoing assessment initiatives in each department. This inventory revealed that while a number of assessment activities were taking place, many needed to be more intentionally focused on student learning. To orient the staff to the idea of the assessment of student learning, a professional development workshop was held with these major items on the agenda:

- Discussion of the difference between assessment of student learning and assessment of student satisfaction,

- Review of assessment efforts already taken in division, and

- Discussion of the five components of an effective assessment process.

After the workshop, the staff was assigned to investigate the kinds of instruments available to them to assess the fulfillment of the core functions (mission and goals) and learning outcomes of their departments. They were also requested to develop an assessment plan to measure their effectiveness in fulfilling their mission and goals and learning outcomes in their departments before the end of that academic year. In a memorandum, the vice president identified the need to include these components of an effective assessment process:

- The needs of our students related to your professional responsibilities

- The use of the services you provide and participation in the programs you offer

- The achievement of your mission, goals and learning outcomes

- Behavior changes in students over time that result from participation in your programs or the use of your services

- Student satisfaction with participation in your programs or the use of your services.

In the following academic year, the outcomes of the *Principles of Good Practice in Student Affairs* assessment exercise were used as the basis of the development of a statement of planning priorities for the Division of Student and Campus Life. The staff agreed upon the following priorities:

- The Student and Campus Life staff will explicitly identify the learning outcomes of the programs and services it sponsors, and routinely assess the usage of its services and their effectiveness in promoting student learning.

- The Student and Campus Life staff will develop relationships that result in the sponsoring of learning oriented programs and services that involve collaboration among staff within and outside the Division and between faculty and staff.

- The Student and Campus Life staff will foster a sense of community that reflects an understanding of the role of the institution's commitment to diversity.

- The Student and Campus Life staff will utilize the College's information technology network and other means to communicate an accurate understanding of the programs and services it offers to students and the commitment of the staff to excellence in program management and to student learning.

- The Student and Campus Life staff will promote involvement in community service and service learning as effective pedagogy consistent with the mission of the College.

- The Student and Campus Life staff will foster community by facilitating an enhanced understanding of the role of Greek life at Geneseo.

ASSESSING THE INTERNAL WORK ENVIRONMENT

The templates that follow are illustrations of tools that can facilitate assessments of the internal work environment. As noted earlier, CAS provides self-assessment guides that can be used to assess more than 30 programs and services in student affairs.

Template A

Self-Assessment of a Student Affairs Practitioner

How do I contribute to student learning at my institution?

How do I contribute to integrated learning at my institution?

Is integrated learning one of my top daily priorities?

One example of an integrated learning program at my institution is _____.

One example of a new program I would like to help establish to promote integrated student learning is _____.

My involvement in integrated learning opportunities on my campus is constrained by my lack of awareness or knowledge of _____.

My involvement in integrated learning on my campus is constrained by the following environmental factors: _____.

In what specific way will I work this year to collaborate with a faculty member to promote integrated learning?

What are the programs that I facilitate that I know (based on research and assessment) contribute to student learning?

What are the programs that I am responsible for that have been shown to have a tenuous impact on student learning?

How do I model a commitment to integrated learning in fulfilling my daily work responsibilities?

Have I taken the initiative to create opportunities to establish and maintain professional relationships with faculty and academic administrators on my campus?

Have I exploited opportunities to demonstrate my interest in and support for faculty work?

Have I thought about what I can offer faculty members to assist them in fulfilling their instructional goals?

Do I facilitate a regular flow of information from my department on the student learning that we facilitate?

Do I regularly analyze institutional data on the student learning that occurs through the program and activities sponsored by my department or area?

Source: Author compilation.

Template B
Self-Assessment of a Faculty Member

How do I contribute to co-curricular student learning at my institution?

One example of an integrated learning program at my institution is _____.

One example of a new program I would like to help establish to promote integrated student learning is _____.

My involvement in integrated learning opportunities on my campus is constrained by these personal factors: _____.

My involvement in integrated learning on my campus is constrained by the following environmental factors: _____.

In what specific way can I work this year to remove a barrier that has prevented me from fostering integrated learning?

In what specific way will I work this year to collaborate with a student affairs staff member to promote integrated learning?

Have I taken the initiative to create opportunities to establish and maintain professional relationships with student affairs administrators on my campus?

Have I exploited opportunities to demonstrate my interest in and support for student affairs work?

Have I thought about what I can offer student affairs members to assist them in fulfilling their educational goals?

Have I evaluated the educational impact of my actions as a club or organization advisor?

Source: Author compilation.

CHAPTER 6
INTEGRATING *LEARNING RECONSIDERED* IN STRATEGIC PLANNING

Richard P. Keeling

INTRODUCTION

Strategic planning should be a process through which departments, divisions, or entire institutions determine the highest and best use of their unique resources to achieve their goals. Strategic planning supports the organization's mission, must be consistent with its vision, and responds to its current and anticipated educational, administrative, political, competitive, and fiscal challenges and opportunities. Strategic planning is, therefore, highly contextual; it is sensitive to current expectations, perceptions, and pressures, and to the availability and flow of resources during any given period of time. The contextual character of strategic planning gives it a relatively short half-life and demands that it be a flexible and adaptable process. Short-term strategic plans (with a three-to-five year lifespan), like short-term weather forecasts, are more reliable and meaningful than longer-term ones.

In many colleges and universities, strategic planning has a bad name. Its legacy is often one of high effort with little return—and, therefore, of low value. Time-demanding meetings, intrusive surveys, and repeated interruptions of routine can make the aftertaste of strategic planning bitter and long lasting. Members of the faculty, administrators, and student affairs professionals often agree that their last voyage into the uncertain and frustrating waters of strategic planning resulted only in a thick report in yet another binder that now occupies space on a sagging shelf.

Strategic planning works when it has purpose, focus, and follow-through; when it has a balance of broad participation and effective leadership; and when it reflects a practical vision that links it at once to aspirations and grounded realities. In the context of *Learning Reconsidered,* strategic planning offers an important opportunity to align vision, mission, goals, objectives, and activities in support of student learning. At the institutional level, it is the way to give life to an emerging campus commitment to use all of a college's resources to support the education and preparation of the whole student. It offers a method for translating a critical but amorphous idea—shared responsibility for learning—into specific decisions about the allocation of scarce resources. It puts money, positions, and priorities into the service of transformative education. With a functioning strategic plan—and an ongoing process of organizational learning and continuous improvement—in place, institutions make themselves accountable for the establishment, assessment, and documentation of student outcomes. Strategy, in other words, becomes both a method of macro-level decision-making and the backbone that gives substance to those decisions.

ADVANCING STUDENT LEARNING THROUGH STRATEGIC PLANNING

Acknowledging the challenge of creating change in higher education, *Learning Reconsidered* was nonetheless clear about the shared responsibility of educators in all colleges and universities:

Regardless of our past accomplishments or disappointments, we are all, as colleagues and educators, now accountable to students and society for identifying and achieving essential student learning outcomes and for making transformative education possible and accessible for all students (p. 3).

The 16 major recommendations in *Learning Reconsidered* name the practical implications of that accountability and provide a framework within which institutional planning can address the greater goal of supporting student learning. The first recommendation calls for a particular approach to strategic planning that would support that goal: "Colleges and universities of every type should commit to the intentional review and strengthening of every institutional structure and resource that can support transformative learning," and the second connects greater institutional purposes to patterns of resource allocation: "Every post-secondary institution should determine and specify its intended student outcomes and should commit resources to measuring, assessing, and documenting students' achievement of those outcomes" (p. 28). Recommendation #5 links strategy to organizational structure: "Senior administrators in academic and student affairs, in partnership with the president of each institution, should review current administrative and organizational structures to determine whether they support the accomplishment of desired student outcomes, and should consider restructuring when necessary to support a strong emphasis on the education of the whole student" (p. 28).

The message in these recommendations is clear: rethink everything, and make sure that structure, resources, and priorities are aligned with accountability for student outcomes. That message establishes the foundation for a form of strategic planning that meets the demands noted earlier.

STRATEGIC PLANNING FOR WHAT?

It is difficult to imagine how a department, division, or whole campus would reorient thought and action to address its accountability for educating and preparing the whole student without questioning existing organizational structures, the current allocation of resources, and established goals and priorities; and the process through which those questions are asked, answered, and linked to future commitments is exactly that of strategic planning. The advantage created by *Learning Reconsidered* is in providing a definite answer to another important question, often asked only covertly and hesitantly as the wheels of strategic planning begin to turn: *strategic planning for what?* Why do we need to do this? What difference will it make? Will we actually get something out of this?

Strategic planning processes fail when they cannot respond meaningfully and convincingly to those questions. When strategic planning seems only to be a mechanical exercise engaged in because it has been a while since the last time it was done, it fails to inspire, motivate, or reward the people involved or the effort that it requires; there is much pain and little gain. Strategic planning also underachieves when it does not deliver, or delivers dysfunctionally, on its promises; assertions that the next strategic planning cycle will "make a real difference this time," if unfulfilled by real results, only create cynicism about the process and raise doubts about the commitments and legitimacy of leaders.

By giving the process something inspiring but tangible to shoot for—supporting transformative learning, specifying and documenting student outcomes, and doing whatever is necessary to support a strong emphasis on the education and preparation of the whole student—the ideas of *Learning Reconsidered* give meaning to strategic planning. They create a *planning concept*—a way of thinking about, focusing, and organizing the work of strategic planning that avoids slippage into semiconscious, humdrum activity.

COMMITMENTS TO PLANNING

The assumption underlying any strategic planning process that intends to bring an organization forward toward supporting transformative learning and being accountable for student outcomes is that leaders are in fact committed to those purposes and willing to act on those commitments. So it is that the first step in establishing a legitimate, authentic planning process is securing and qualifying the commitments of leaders. There is absolutely no point in setting in motion resource-intensive, potentially disruptive planning processes that have no chance of implementation; in fact, doing so only undermines morale and wastes time and energy.

Qualifying commitments means establishing that statements are backed by real intentions, which in turn means that leaders understand the implications of the commitments they are making. A commitment to strategic planning in support of the goals advocated in *Learning Reconsidered* means a commitment to significant operational, structural, and organizational change; to reallocating resources, if necessary, to support change; and to accepting accountability for both establishing and assessing student outcomes.

The depth and resonance of these implications differs, of course, depending on the scope of the planning process; a department head or director can commit to change more easily than a senior student affairs officer or a president. But the core point of supporting transformative learning is that doing so involves "every institutional structure and resource" (*Learning Reconsidered*, p. 28); department heads and directors need to ensure that their planning activities are aligned with the intentions of the division; and the senior student affairs officer has to synchronize planning with the ideas and commitments of the president, who in turn is accountable to the governing board. All of which means that initiating strategic planning using the rubrics and concepts of *Learning Reconsidered* requires a pre-planning phase of significant and honest discussion that prepares leaders at every level to realize what this kind of planning process entails and what it could produce. Without such discussion, planning is likely to proceed at cross purposes and could generate real risks to the department, division, or institution.

LINKING STUDENT OUTCOMES WITH STRATEGIC PLANNING

Since establishing student learning outcomes (for departments, divisions, and the entire campus) and implementing assessment processes to measure and document achievement of them are essential elements of accountability for supporting student learning, the work of developing learning outcomes is now often linked with, or embedded in, strategic planning. Many divisions of student affairs have adopted learning outcomes as the model within which to begin or restructure their planning activities.

Developing student learning outcomes and assessment methods is itself a broadly participatory planning process that requires close examination of the purposes and effects of programs, services, and activities. In Chapter 4, Komives and Schoper describe guidelines and approaches to writing learning outcomes; here, it is important to note that the process through which student affairs professionals or members of the faculty learn to do so demands attention and resources. Learning to "do" student learning outcomes means learning a new language, thinking differently about day-to-day activities, renewing relationships with colleagues and students, and adopting the assumptions and values of a culture of assessment. Most educators—in the faculty or student affairs—do not arrive pre-wired to do the things that learning outcomes require.

Two key steps are necessary, then, to prepare educators to define and document learning outcomes: (1) professional development and training—often called *capacity building*—to increase their ability to write learning outcomes, create assessment plans, use assessment methods and tools, and prepare reports that document the work; and (2) a cultural adaptation that shapes the attitudes, perspectives, and working styles necessary for effective use of outcomes and assessment techniques. These two steps intersect and inform each other throughout the process of preparation. In most institutions, and in most circumstances, building the capacity of staff members to write and assess learning outcomes is an iterative process that takes at least a full academic year, and often longer. It requires education, collaboration, and, above all else, practice, with a great deal of personal mentoring; and staff members need to become comfortable in a group working relationship characterized by productive, constructive feedback and mutual goal setting. What staff members learn to do and the ways in which they learn to work together through the learning outcomes process will support contemporaneous or subsequent strategic planning activities very effectively. Working with learning outcomes and designing and implementing assessment plans are activities that have both strategic and tactical elements—and an advantage created by focusing on learning outcomes in the setting of strategic planning is that everyone involved learns to tell the difference between the two.

Borrego, in Chapter 3, reflects on the concern expressed by some student affairs professionals that a learning outcomes model does not effectively describe, represent, or document their work. Especially in service-oriented operations (recreation centers, unions, and clinical health programs, for example), staff members may feel that efficiency, student satisfaction, and numbers of encounters or interactions are more meaningful and accurate measures of their work. But, as Borrego notes, these services exist for the specific reason that they support learning and enhance the student experience—because, in other words, they advance the academic mission of the institution, either by directly promoting learning (for example, through training for student employees) or by removing or reducing barriers to academic achievement (such as physical or psychological health problems).

Measures of student affairs professionals' effectiveness in delivering services (often called institutional, or operational, effectiveness indicators) are important, and should be used in parallel with student learning outcomes. But it is wrong to believe that learning does not happen, or cannot be assessed, in those programs and services. And it is wrong to think that those services should not be part of strategic planning processes that focus on achieving student learning outcomes and educating the whole student.

ALIGNING STRUCTURE, RESOURCES, AND PRIORITIES WITH ACCOUNTABILITY FOR STUDENT OUTCOMES

The purpose of this chapter is not to explicate the steps in strategic planning; there are many resources available that provide advice and guidance to leaders and staff members about ways to do strategic planning effectively and economically. But it is important to explore some points about strategic planning in the context of an institutional commitment to support student learning.

- **Leadership of the process is critical to success.** The range of organizational, structural, programmatic, and operational options open to consideration as departments, divisions, and campuses seek to emphasize the education of the whole student and support and document student learning is extremely broad. Leaders have the responsibility of reminding participants in the process that existing structures and systems have usually not supported those goals, and of encouraging not only innovative thinking, but also purposeful reconsideration of every aspect of the organization's work. In other words, leaders have to give permission for participants to address topics and propose strategies that might in previous planning processes have been considered "off limits" or improper.

- **Focus, focus, focus.** A clear, streamlined focus on student learning and student outcomes—not contaminated by other priorities—will produce better results. If making transformative learning accessible for every student is our priority (and it should be), then every strategy that emerges from the planning process should be focused on supporting that goal.

- **Form and function are inseparable.** It is unlikely that strategies that separate activities from structures will succeed. If goals drive strategies, and strategies drive activities, then structures have to follow; structures (including administrative and organizational relationships, reporting lines, and the basic organizational map of the institution itself) are ways of supporting activities that match resources to needs. In other words, structures are not ends in themselves. So installing a process of developing and assessing learning outcomes, for example, without questioning whether existing organizations, positions, and working relationships can support that process does not make sense.

- **Not everything is from the ground up.** A fixture of current strategic planning efforts on campuses is a commitment to a community-based, participatory process. Without countering that sanguine trend or suggesting that the idea of broad participation is in any way ill-conceived, it is nonetheless equally important to note that high level strategy development requires as much a macroscopic view as a grassroots one. Robert Frost, who probably never thought about institutional strategic planning or student learning outcomes, wrote a line that pertains to the need for balance between "ground up" and leadership-oriented elements in planning: "It is hard to see the field from within the field." Organizational change often requires considering strategies that will not be obvious—or appealing—

to staff members who work "in the field." Organizational change also often requires considering other strategies that would not have occurred to—and may not immediately appeal to—senior leaders. Both perspectives are necessary. Without one, planning becomes impractical and ungrounded; without the other, it too easily lapses into tactical or incremental planning.

- **Account for satisfaction and effectiveness, but emphasize outcomes.** Another predictable component of strategic planning has become the satisfaction survey—an assessment of the degree to which students, faculty, staff, and other constituents are pleased with the direction, operations, programs, and services of the institution (or of a particular division, department, or program). The information provided through these surveys is pertinent and should be embraced—but kept in perspective. The movement toward outcomes is explicitly a shift *away from* a reliance on satisfaction indicators as the primary way to set priorities and plan the allocation of resources. The premise of this shift is that, in the long term, outcomes matter more in higher education than immediate indicators of satisfaction. It is a chronic, growing frustration with the utility and value of short-term measures of satisfaction that fuels the growing protest on campuses about rankings of colleges in popular magazines and drives concern about the growth of institutional investments in marketing, competition, and branding. If outcomes are the priority, and if outcomes are achieved, students (and parents and other constituents) will have abundant reasons to be satisfied. But if there are no clear student outcomes for a campus or if those outcomes are not produced, ultimately no one will be satisfied.

- **Big questions motivate good thinking.** The traditional SWOT (strengths, weaknesses, opportunities, and threats) analysis can be made pertinent to strategic planning that is conducted with student learning goals in mind, but it is unwise to *start* the process that way. Instead, start with big questions, such as: What would it mean to have every resource and structure of our organization support transformative learning? What characteristics of our administrative structure make it harder for us to emphasize education of the whole student? What barriers are created by our customary ways of operating? What obstacles impede our ability to make the whole campus a learning community?

- **Identify professional development and training needs.** A strong strategic planning process entails serious consideration of implementation requirements, including professional development and training. What new skills and abilities do staff members need to participate fully and productively in the activities that would support the proposed objectives and goals of the plan? Especially, what specific capacity building is needed to make linkages between learning outcomes and the strategic planning process—including implementation—strong and successful?

- **Stop, or keep going.** A common piece of advice-giving about strategic planning is to suggest that planning is (a) not an end in itself, and (b) not a project that ends at some definite point in the near future. "Strategic planning is a *process*," it goes, and it does not end with the writing and dissemination of the plan itself. True enough, all of that, and the need for continuous feedback from assessment processes validates the idea that organizations should never plan to stop planning. But it is also true that the cycles of development and assessment of student outcomes are longer than a single academic year; strategic planning in the context of student outcomes will have a cyclic, phased character, and is likely to be less linear than ordinary strategic planning processes.

CONCLUSION

The ideas and concepts of *Learning Reconsidered* provide an apt and constructive framework, or model, for implementing strategic planning in departments, divisions, or whole institutions. Infusing those ideas and concepts influences the character, prospects, and methods of strategic planning and can enhance the motivation and strengthen the contributions of participants in the process. At the same time, using student outcomes and transformative learning as the conceptual basis for strategic planning creates certain important requirements and implications for the process. Linking the development and assessment of student learning outcomes to strategic planning can strengthen the planning work but requires upfront investments in capacity building through training and professional development.

CHAPTER 7
ENHANCING PROFESSIONAL DEVELOPMENT

Susan Borrego
Cynthia Forrest
Jane Fried

INTRODUCTION

Whenever we begin to think about changing our frame of reference for our professional work, our first question must be, "What skills, cognitive abilities, and knowledge do we need in order to move the desired change forward?" And then, "How can we maximize progress, and minimize resistance?" Our professional development activities are one place in which we begin to address these questions.

The change in frame of reference occurring within the academy to refocus on learning outcomes linked with student success provides a unifying framework for the work of all campus educators. What knowledge and skills do we need to participate as equal partners with members of the faculty in that work? How can professional development programs in student affairs help prepare us?

Historically, our educational practice has emphasized information transfer without much thought given to meaning, pertinence, or application of information in the context of a student's life (*Learning Reconsidered*, 2004, p. 10). Advancing an integrated approach to learning requires a collaborative framework for working with colleagues throughout campus (for more discussion about the importance and creation of collaborative relationships, please see Chapter 9). To achieve the goals of an integrated approach that supports student learning, everyone within the academy must be invited to engage in a collaborative process.

Donald Schön (1982) describes this as a deeply reflective process to consider our assumptions, the transformative practices, new alliances, and creative approaches that will bolster and support student learning and success. Such a commitment to student learning and success requires that student affairs practitioners consider new ways of thinking about our work on each campus and engage in new types of professional development.

SUPPORTING STUDENT LEARNING REQUIRES DIFFERENT PROFESSIONAL DEVELOPMENT ACTIVITIES

Our assumptions about student learning and the role of student affairs have seldom been examined. Now we must be willing to unpack our assumptions about the nature and substance of our professional practice and explore in more depth the ways in which we do, or could, advance student learning and promote student success in our own institutional contexts. We need flexible skills that will allow us to operate at multiple levels when focusing on student learning; our assumptions and past experiences may not serve us well if we import them into our current work and superimpose them on present day campus culture. In order to work differently in and outside of our own divisions, we must be intentional learners and reflective practitioners, learning continuously about our campus and our students, thinking about the way our work addresses the demands of institutional mission and values, and committed to examining and revising our operational assumptions about student learning. Most of us will have to update our professional development activities and reconsider the requisite skills for creating successful learning environments.

PRIMARY AREAS FOR SKILL DEVELOPMENT

We have identified three primary areas for developing skills that will advance the vision of *Learning Reconsidered* and strengthen student learning: collaboration, leadership, and an understanding of strategies for organizational development and change.

- **Collaboration.** Often what we describe as "collaborative" is actually simply cooperative. Sharing timelines, reporting on programs, and aligning calendars are all useful activities but do not in and of themselves usually lead to deep and sustained collaborative efforts. For example, staff will often come to divisional meetings with a calendar of events to share with colleagues; informing colleagues of forthcoming events is certainly cooperative, but not necessarily collaborative practice. But if we started as a whole staff with divisional learning outcomes and planned strategies to accomplish and demonstrate those outcomes, we would have a very different kind of conversation.

  Collaborative planning has the additional benefit of becoming a professional development activity in itself as the participants learn to understand the worldviews and work of their partners. Collaboration requires a particular set of skills, which may come naturally to some and can be learned by others. These skills include the ability to understand the perspectives of others, the capacity to engage in dialogue, and the ability to build on others' ideas.

  Collaboration, in contrast to more simple kinds of cooperation, requires mutual goal setting and development of programs and activities. For example, if a campus decides to develop a residential learning community,

the learning goals and activities should be integrated and supported by the department of residential life and the academic departments involved. Professors must begin by developing the curriculum together and by working with the residential life staff to integrate experiential activities that support the goals of the community. Different kinds of skills (and sometimes, different staffing patterns) may be required of the residential life staff. If each group works separately, even though they are willing to cooperate, additional time will be required to connect all parts of the program after segmented planning has occurred.

- **Leadership.** Becoming an invitational leader, as described by Segal and Purkey (2002) in their book, *Becoming an Invitational Leader—A New Approach to Professional and Personal Success*, requires that aspiring leaders consider "the total environment in which a leader functions" and suggests that "the Invitational Leader is unique in asking others to meet their goals as a condition of his or her own success" (p. 23). Leadership that helps others develop an understanding of student-centered learning and the multiple locations of student learning is critical, no matter what role or position one holds in an organization (such as supervising student staff, managing professional staff, or working with faculty collaborators).

  There are at least two dimensions to consider in the area of leadership that promote student learning and success. The first element centers on each professional's internal motivation for professional growth in these areas, and the second addresses the external leadership required to marshal resources and institute policies and professional practices designed to advance student learning. In both instances, leadership that is purposeful, intentional and inviting leads to an individual and collective focus on explicit outcomes and strategic actions. This type of leadership emphasizes that one's individual learning requires personal and organizational commitments that invite a deeper understanding of students and of the dynamic nature of the institution's mission, constraints and opportunities related to student learning.

Selecting readings, conference sessions, mentoring opportunities, and relationship development that increase one's understanding in these areas are priorities for individual professional development. Given the current institutional, fiscal, and, sometimes, legislative constraints for travel, individual professionals must often invest personal resources in this endeavor. But every division of student affairs should be accountable for encouraging and fostering the professional development of members of its staff.

- **Organizational Development and Change.**
Another very important element of today's professional development requirements is organizational transformation and structural change. Professionals must develop an understanding of change to be in a position to help institutions reach their goals of transformative learning.

Transformative environments are sustained by those who can navigate chaos and set a course for the institution to become a *learning organization* (Senge and Associates, 1994). Learning organizations develop the capacity to gather feedback on their own effectiveness, absorb new information into the decision-making structure, and compare the outcomes of their activities with their espoused goals. The culture of the organization changes through the commitment of members to see the organization as a whole and to change their behavioral and organizational patterns to support the goals of the organization (Wheatley, 1999).

Rather than bristle about the inevitable occurrence of change (whether planned or unanticipated), staff in successful organizations must learn from change and find ways to explore the opportunities that it can create. Rather than advancing competitive goals as defined by subgroups in the institution, they spend time trying to articulate common goals, even if all goals in each department are not related to the goals of other departments. Learning organizations look for areas in which collaboration will lead to improved ability to achieve institutional goals. Intentionally assisting the organization to support student learning at all levels necessitates professionals who understand the complexity of change and can facilitate the process.

Deciding that the focus of an institution should be on student learning and mapping the learning sites so that all learning can be integrated are complex actions with many prerequisites and consequences. The outcomes are ambiguous, and the history of teaching and learning is long and entrenched. In addition, there are job descriptions, union contracts, different kinds of values and skills, very different understandings of what it means to teach, learn and assess learning, different investments of institutional resources and extremely different working conditions for people in different segments of the institution.

Transforming the entire focus of an institution is a process of culture change, and that never happens quickly; we need both the ability to conceive and map organizational change, and the attitudes and skills necessary to recognize and exploit opportunities for change.

SKILLS TO MOVE FORWARD

Greater Expectations "challenges all stake-holders to unite for collective action, creating a coherent educational system designed to help all students achieve the greater expectations that are the hallmark of our time." (2002, iv. Preface). What skills, abilities and knowledge do we need to recognize and exploit opportunities for change?

We need *dialogue skills*, the ability to bring groups together to help them articulate common goals for learning and to design programs that support that goal in a variety of contexts, across numerous learning styles (Kolb, 1984) and kinds of intelligences. We need the ability to bring people together and to conduct conversations in which all participants feel that they are being heard and understood. In these conversations, we need to manage relationships in which there are power differentials, and we need to draw in people who are not usually invited. Just as the faculty members are the knowledge experts, the student affairs staff needs to become the dialogue experts.

COGNITIVE ABILITIES AND KNOWLEDGE

What cognitive abilities and knowledge do we need to transform our institutional environments, and move them in the direction of collaboration in support of learning?

1. We need the ability to understand who the stakeholders are when we think that a new approach to a learning issue is necessary. Which departments have a stake in the process when a First Year Experience course is being designed, for example? Who stands to gain students, and who stands to lose students and financial resources? It is possible that some paid workers may lose their jobs because of an influx of volunteers as an unintended consequence of a new service learning program? Do these workers need some additional training in order to supervise or work with the student volunteers?

When student affairs staff members or departments ask to be included in first year experience programs, do they understand the faculty culture that they are entering and may be disrupting? What do student affairs staff members need to know before they enter another culture, even one on their own campus?

2. We need the same ability to understand the vested interests of the departments that are involved in some shift of responsibilities, such as moving academic advising, admissions, career counseling and financial aid into an enrollment management department. Although this shift may seem very reasonable from a number of different perspectives and may help students succeed far more frequently than under the previous system, do the decision-makers really understand the implications and consequences of such a shift? Do the staff members in each formerly separate office understand? Would the change work better if there were some dialogue between offices before such a shift is made? All of these questions involve large amounts of information and extremely complicated transactions. What do the decision-makers need to know and how do they need to think about it in order to make this shift work for students and staff?

3. We need the ability to gather and analyze data about learning needs and a host of other needs, resources, institutional priorities and outcomes. Collaboration is key to developing this set of skills. Most campuses have faculty or staff members who are expert in various aspects of research, data collection, and data analysis. The experts may be in departments of psychology, sociology or institutional research. Many student affairs professionals do not believe that they

have these skill sets and may be somewhat wary about learning them.

CONCLUSION

An intentional focus in student affairs on active collaboration to advance student learning requires new knowledge, cognitive tools, and skills. The capacity to collaborate with other professionals (in or out of student affairs, and on or off campus—but especially, in the faculty) is central to our success, and responsible student affairs programs will focus professional development resources on improvements in the skills, attitudes, and knowledge base necessary for effective collaboration. Leadership skills are also essential, and the ability to organize and support organizational change is a key skill of leaders. New cognitive skills needed for the next generation of student affairs professionals include understanding and managing data and interpreting qualitative, or narrative material from conversations with academic departments. Professional development activities can be focused on these needs and concerns.

CHAPTER 8
PUTTING *LEARNING RECONSIDERED* INTO PRACTICE

Richard H. Mullendore

INTRODUCTION

Learning Reconsidered has generated considerable excitement among student affairs professionals, but concerns have been raised regarding how to put the concepts, ideas and recommendations into practice. This chapter is designed to ensure that *Learning Reconsidered* will not become just another publication to place on the shelf, but that it will become a living document that may create a revolution in higher education.

Cynics may argue that *Learning Reconsidered* is the most recent attempt by the student affairs profession to level the playing field with their academic counterparts at a time when the profession is struggling to maintain its (rightful) place at the president's table. At many institutions, the division of student affairs is moving administratively to become a subset of academic affairs, and no longer reporting to the president. What should then be an incredible opportunity for academic affairs/student affairs collaboration, however, often becomes a reduction in status, authority and influence. Provosts may seem to be more interested in faculty matters, credit hour production, numbers of students in majors, recruitment issues, research funding, and the number of books in the library than in opportunities for student learning and development in student leadership programs, Greek life, residence hall living/learning centers, student activities, recreation programs, career centers, etc. At the same time, presidents are being chosen from outside higher education in greater numbers than ever before and many are primarily concerned with fund raising, political issues, and institutional image.

To turn adversity into advocacy, it is important to be able to articulate what is different about *Learning Reconsidered* and to understand what separates this document from other great student affairs literature. How far have we come from the 1937 *Student Personnel Point of View* (American Council on Education, 1937)? What advances have been made in understanding learning since Robert Brown's (1972) *Student Development in Higher Education—A Return to the Academy*? How does this document fit with the criticisms of Bloland, Stamatakos, and Rogers (1994) in *Reform in Student Affairs*? Why should this document supercede *The Student Learning Imperative: Implications for Student Affairs (1994)*?

The simple answer about what is different is that *Learning Reconsidered* has put academic learning and student development processes together in a format that requires all the resources of the academy to function together in an integrated manner on behalf of students. The challenge to implementation is gaining consensus that student learning is so important that faculty, staff, and administrators will be willing to climb outside the comfort of their silos and reinvent higher education.

CRITICAL ISSUES IN IMPLEMENTATION

Among the greatest barriers to implementation are the people who can make a difference. Presidential vision, support and encouragement, beyond words alone, are the most critical factors for success. What is the background and what are the previous experiences of your president? How does this person view student affairs? Are you seen as service providers for customers, student development specialists, or partners in learning? Is student affairs at the table each week or is there a filter between student affairs and the president? Who is the chief academic officer, and what does this individual see as appropriate roles for student affairs? The provost or academic vice president is often the primary gatekeeper for student affairs involvement (which may be perceived as intrusion) into the academic life of students. To be successful, this person must hear and understand the president's message of support and be willing to commit time, clout, and resources to the effort.

How decentralized is your institution? Do academic deans operate with a high degree of independence? Is faculty development important to them? Is teaching truly an important variable in the promotion and tenure process? To be successful, deans must be supportive of collaborative efforts of their faculty outside specific disciplines. Do faculty members have a tradition of collaboration with student affairs? Are they engaged with students outside the classroom on a regular basis? Without faculty energy and support, implementation of the principles espoused in *Learning Reconsidered* is destined for failure.

What are the academic credentials, previous experiences, and institutional credibility of the chief student affairs officer (CSAO)? Do staff members in the student affairs division have a history of seeking to engage individual faculty in their work? Are student affairs staff appropriately credentialed, competent in their work, and committed to the long term success of programs in their institution?

Most successful educational revolutions begin with a visionary champion. Who will be the champion of student learning on your campus? Chief student affairs officers are clearly well-positioned to lead the effort. With support of the president and the chief academic officer, the CSAO can articulate the vision at every opportunity from new student orientation to new faculty orientation to faculty departmental meetings to the community beyond the institution. Today's emphasis on outcomes and

persistence provide a wonderful stage from which to operate, and student affairs has generally been at the forefront of these initiatives.

BEGINNING TO IMPLEMENT *LEARNING RECONSIDERED*

The potential for success in implementing *Learning Reconsidered* recommendations is enhanced by trying pilot programs, engaging one faculty member at a time, and persisting in the vision. Becoming a transformative learning community is a process, not an event. It requires time, energy, resources, patience and tenacity. As your institution moves toward implementation, it may be helpful to begin with some time-tested pilot programs where campus systems and networks can easily and successfully collaborate.

For those colleges with residence halls, residential academic initiatives can build upon an existing student affairs infrastructure. Providing opportunities for faculty to live-in can be a wonderful win/win for both students and faculty members. These faculty members bring the learning environment "home" with them every day. Students learn to develop relationships with faculty outside the classroom, and opportunities to reflect on classroom learning are abundant.

An expansion of this effort is the development of residential colleges where students select a residence hall, or portion thereof, based on their major and the live-in faculty member teaches in that major. An example is a Spanish language hall where only Spanish is spoken in the common areas, and where faculty can provide programs to enhance the learning experience. Satellite counseling centers and academic advising centers can be developed in residence halls to assist students in making meaning of their college experiences and to plan their academic programs in an informal setting.

Service learning experiences, appropriately structured, provide one of the most effective student affairs and academic affairs collaborations to transform and integrate the learning and reflection processes. Divisions of student affairs have had community volunteer programs in place for years, and some have reached out to faculty to make service learning a course component. These programs provide an excellent opportunity to integrate classroom learning with real world issues and allow students to reflect on their learning.

A few years ago, an investment firm ran an ad campaign saying they built their business one investor at a time. This concept works well with student affairs/faculty collaborations as well. Every college has faculty members who will readily agree with and support the recommendations in *Learning Reconsidered*. A key in implementation is to engage those faculty members, one person at a time, to commit to a partnership to make a few of the recommendations a reality within their sphere of influence. Success breeds success and others will follow. It is important that mechanisms be in place to market successful ventures so that the entire campus community is informed. Letters of thanks to committed faculty with copies to the dean, provost and president are important.

BEYOND INITIAL IMPLEMENTATION

Persisting in the vision is perhaps the most critical component for success in implementation of the *Learning Reconsidered* recommendations.

How can a division of student affairs sustain the momentum of successful collaborative learning programs when staff attrition is an ongoing concern? Faculty members, for the most part, tend to stay at their institutions for long periods, perhaps their entire careers; whereas student affairs staff members are much more transitory in their careers, which may inhibit faculty participation in new initiatives. The CSAOs, provosts, and presidents (although often temporary themselves) must work tirelessly to routinize successful learning collaborations, so initiatives continue after staff or administrators depart. Responding to today's emphasis on outcomes and assessment should be helpful to institutions that desire to continue to build upon the *Learning Reconsidered* momentum.

Putting the concepts and recommendations outlined in *Learning Reconsidered* into practice should be a priority for every division of student affairs. This document is not designed to gather dust on a shelf; it is as important as the CAS Standards to our work. Implementation of the recommendations does not tread on sacred academic territory; it is our responsibility to do everything we can to enhance the learning environment, and *Learning Reconsidered* provides a wonderful roadmap to help us along the way.

CHAPTER 9
CREATING STRATEGIES FOR COLLABORATION

Jeanne Steffes
Richard P. Keeling

INTRODUCTION

Learning Reconsidered argued for the integrated use of all of higher education's resources in the education and preparation of the whole student. One of the most critical elements required to accomplish this is the creation or enhancement of strong, collaborative working relationships among academic and student affairs educators. Many of the most pressing recommendations in *Learning Reconsidered* are situated in, and dependent on, the development of respectful collaboration between these historically segregated divisions; generative collaboration will serve as the infrastructure for all subsequent discussions, projects, programs and activities. It is crucial that these structural and functional working relationships be intentionally and thoughtfully developed, adequately resourced, and strategically maintained to promote the best outcomes. In today's environment in higher education, resources continue to decrease, while the demand for an educated population increases; collaboration has become more essential and the need to understand, support, and manage it will continue to grow.

WHY COLLABORATION MATTERS

The advantages of a collaborative approach may seem obvious in the context of reform in higher education, and they are assumed in the work of *Learning Reconsidered*. It is, however, worth noting that:

- Collaboration makes better use of all the available talent; in higher education as in business, it is increasingly the way that work gets done.

- Collaboration reorients and links resources in ways that make the total value of them greater than the sum of their parts.

- Collaboration forms a network of ideas and resources that not only supports student learning, but also creates a collegial infrastructure that will facilitate institution-wide planning and assessment activities, including preparation for accreditation.

- Through collaboration, we develop a mutual language and shared assumptions about the value, importance, and support of student learning; this makes it possible for faculty and student affairs educators to think together, in common terms, about students and their needs and to imagine campus-wide efforts to enhance their experience and promote their learning.

- Collaboration creates a spectrum of new and healthy cultural norms that can transform working relationships and re-focus energy away from competition and the maintenance of silos and toward cross-functional planning and shared responsibility for learning.

A failure to collaborate can produce contrary outcomes:

- The perpetuation of territorial attitudes, a "silo mentality," and competition for scarce resources.

- Continuation of a fractured, segregated approach to students and learning in which the intellect is valued and addressed differently from the whole person.

- More divided, and therefore less, total attention to students and their experience.

- Poor utilization of resources—including the insufficient recognition and deployment of all the available talent among faculty and staff.

- Greater perceived isolation of the institution from major social, business, and cultural trends; consequently, less effective preparation of students for the world of work and civic participation. Students educated in institutions that do not value or support collaboration will likely be less capable of working in teams, recognizing and responding to the gifts and ideas of others, and learning in multiple contexts.

- Ineffective stewardship of the public trust and of the resources invested in higher education.

COLLABORATION BETWEEN FACULTY AND STUDENT AFFAIRS EDUCATORS

Learning Reconsidered describes a common group of collaborative interventions that bring together faculty and student affairs educators:

These "powerful partnerships," jointly planned, combine knowledge acquisition and experiential learning to promote more complex outcomes. They include living-learning programs, career development, service learning, academic advising, cultural

identity development, internships, study abroad, film festivals, honor code and academic integrity processes, campus media, culture festivals, and support services for students with disabilities (p. 20).

Learning Reconsidered also describes collaborative initiatives that, while focused primarily on academic outcomes, depend also on the work of student affairs educators:

These opportunities are primarily the responsibility of faculty and other academic affairs educators. They include classroom knowledge acquisition, laboratory and small group research, capstone courses, literary magazines, art exhibits, drama, theater and music productions, and academic clubs (p. 20).

Given our current understanding of learning, collaboration between faculty and student affairs educators is not simply an intelligent option; it is a core requirement for the effective development and achievement of desired student learning outcomes (see Kellogg, 1999). Transformative learning occurs in known cycles and situations (see Fried's discussion in Chapter 2); both the unconscious processing of new material and the intentional or happenstance application and testing of knowledge will, more likely than not, occur outside the classroom and laboratory, in the active context of students' lives. Thinking separately of curriculum and co-curriculum has only administrative value; it is, in fact, counterproductive to continue working with those terms and the assumptions that underlie them.

While the differentiation of educators into two groups (faculty and staff) will almost certainly persist for historic, structural, and political reasons, collaboration between those groups must be assumed, planned, and supported, and ideas, policies, and actions that emphasize or reinforce the division of campuses (and learning) into completely segregated cultures (the proverbial two sides of the house) must be challenged and resisted. As *Learning Reconsidered* suggests, the argument for supporting transformative learning leads, eventually, to a reconsideration of the most basic assumptions in the academy—including current structures and organizational patterns, such as the separation of academic and student affairs. Over time, those structures and patterns will likely be questioned and, on some campuses, revised; already, a few sentinel institutions have reworked the relationship of academic and student affairs educators at an organizational level to support greater collaboration. As Mullendore notes in Chapter 8, some of those restructuring efforts have created more distance (filters) between student affairs and the president (and, therefore, between students and the president). But others are creative experiments, such as the merger of academic and student affairs at the University of North Carolina-Asheville, that reflect steps toward reorganizing institutions to support an integrated approach to student learning.

The advantages of such an approach at an institutional level are a subset of the cluster of points in favor of collaboration noted earlier. There are also distinct advantages for student learning and the student experience. Retention, for example, is a complex phenomenon with multiple determinants, not all of them "academic" or cognitive; the reasons for premature departure from school in most institutions are not primarily academic failure. Students may not continue in school for any number of reasons embedded in their net experience as students at a particular time in a particular institution; some of those reasons may, in fact, have little to do with the institution itself (family problems, health concerns, financial limitations) but might be addressed through the creative use of institutional resources.

The common complaint among departing students (lack of a good fit between them and the college) is itself a simple explanation of a multi-factorial deficiency; preventing or remediating the causes of such a perception is, in most cases, not purely an academic or co-curricular matter. Some students who might have departed will stay in school when faculty and student affairs educators collaborate to discover and address the causes of the student's dissatisfaction or underperformance.

In other chapters there are examples of the possibilities and educational benefits of such collaboration. None of the seven major student outcomes advocated in *Learning Reconsidered* can be accomplished in the classroom alone; none of them can be achieved without the classroom. When specific, institution-wide student outcomes are identified and developed, both academic and student affairs educators must participate. Recent literature contains, for example, helpful discussion of the opportunities created by living learning communities (Stevenson and associates, 2005) and other out-of-classroom learning activities (Steffes, 2004). Both faculty and student affairs educators generally find the experience of collaboration to be both satisfying and energizing; to introduce new ideas about pedagogy and best educational practices; to inspire innovation; and to produce greater understanding of each others' work.

Advocating collaboration is not dismissing its challenges. Disciplinary faculty and student affairs practitioners were prepared for their work in different systems, using different assumptions. The primacy of discovering, creating, and adapting knowledge guides the work of most faculty members; depending on the characteristics and values of the institution, that work may be done in greater or less proximity to the process of student learning. In the lives of some faculty members, the greatest good is effective teaching, through which students come to share the joy of knowledge; for others, teaching is a lower priority, conceived mostly as a service function for undergraduates (but as a welcome, if not emphasized, concomitant of research with graduate students). To the extent that the positivist assumptions discussed by Fried (Chapter 2) pertain, faculty are less likely than their colleagues in student affairs to manifest interest in the student experience; this is not to say that many positivist faculty do not care about students—they do—but, instead, it is a claim about the degree to which those faculty members embrace students as partners and co-creators of the learning experience.

Much discussion about the different reward systems of tenure track faculty, especially, and student affairs professionals has more than made the point that untenured faculty members often cannot afford the diversion or distraction that collaboration might entail; that point is only underscored by the common institutional experience of having a few dedicated faculty members who, by being the exception to the rule, are also over-used in collaborative programs. Student affairs educators are (also unfortunately) often evaluated on the basis of students' reaction to and satisfaction with their work (rather than by reference to their success in advancing student learning and enhancing the student experience); in most colleges and universities, students' ratings of faculty members have little effect on promotion and tenure decisions. Stevenson and associates (2005) note the important feature of "teacher cohesion" inherent in faculty collaboration in student learning interventions—participation gives professors new colleagues and helps overcome their own sense of isolation, and also brings them closer to students in ways that enlarge the sphere of interest in student success. But the relative value of that benefit will be, in each faculty member's experience, weighed against other demands and expectations that may be more closely linked to academic advancement.

The degree to which these differences prevent effective collaboration varies extensively, and is greatly influenced by both institutional culture and leadership; strong advocacy for collaboration, a culture of investment in students, and firm, consistent leadership can transform those differences into opportunities to realign resources in the service of a greater common goal. Conversely, the lack of any of those factors permits differences between faculty and student affairs educators to be magnified into impossible barriers.

Finally, it is important to acknowledge that collaboration has costs as well as benefits. Most colleges and universities are environments of limited resources, and the time, energy, focus, and money needed to invest in building collaborative relationships may be expensive. Collaboration without good communication is especially costly; students may perceive the learning interventions that emerge in those conditions as fragmented, disconnected, and irrelevant. Student affairs professionals whose desire to collaborate is so strong that it overwhelms their commitment to students may make poor decisions with harmful administrative, educational, and organizational consequences. Collaboration requires both respectful acknowledgment of mutual strengths and the maintenance of enough professional distance to avoid losing the essential focus of each of the collaborators. Peter Magolda (2005), emphasizing that collaboration must begin with the partners knowing themselves, not the other, has recently written about the need for caution as well as enthusiasm in developing collaborative relationships between academic and student affairs educators.

CREATING A CULTURE OF COLLABORATION

Fundamentally, the effort to support collaboration is a process of cultural change. The extent and pace of that change must be adapted specifically and carefully—even delicately—to each campus. Collaboration is the kind of cultural phenomenon that, if forced, becomes illegitimate and superficial; if pretended, becomes hard to sustain. The distance between current organizational patterns and desired ones will be far greater in some institutions than others. While there will be in every case exceptions that prove the general rule, the following are suggestions for beginning the process of cultural transformation to support greater collaboration:

- **Start small:** Collaboration, at the outset, does not mean having every faculty member and every student affairs professional equally involved. Good results from attempts at massive reorganizations of working relationships on campus are unlikely.

- **Identify and support champions—but avoid overdependence:** Many professors will commit to pilot programs or trials of innovative learning activities (as long as the reasons for and intended results of their participation are clear; see discussion in Chapter 4). The probability of collaboration increases in direct proportion to the finiteness of the commitment; the more open-ended a request is, the less comfortable and safe a professor may feel in accepting it. And a larger number of professors will agree to time-limited collaboration than unscheduled terms. Developing limited and well-planned collaboration also allows professors to cycle back into their usual and customary roles after participating—thereby opening up space for other professors and avoiding the all-too-common liability of wearing out a sympathetic and helpful professor (who, after a period of overextension, resigns from collaboration and never returns). Rewards never hurt; recognizing and celebrating the successes of effective collaborators reinforces their commitment, creates an attractive opportunity to market collaboration to others, and suggests a model that can inspire imitation (Pollard, 2004).

- **Focus on real problems, not theoretical opportunities:** Professors are more likely to respond to specific requests to work with student affairs professionals on a particular project (that has, as suggested earlier, a timeframe and intended deliverables) than to engage in unstructured or open-ended projects with nonspecific outcomes.

- **Initiate the conversation:** Some student affairs professionals protest the assumption

that they must begin building the bridge of collaboration; "Why don't the faculty come to us," they say. Some professors have, and do, and will. To suppose that all faculty are unconscious about students and student learning is an insulting error. Many faculty members are deeply interested in improving pedagogy, enhancing student learning, and embracing students as partners in learning. But student affairs educators have, as part of their preparation and skill set, a good understanding of the processes of networking, relationship building, and linking resources; they are, most often, in a better position than faculty members to initiate the dialogue.

- **Expect and manage conflict:** Cultures do not change without conflict; creating a culture of collaboration will not be possible without it. As Magolda (2005) suggests, student affairs educators intending to collaborate with faculty should prepare for and embrace conflict, rather than avoiding it, and should be prepared to discuss—and advocate for—their unique contributions to learning.

- **Evaluate the outcomes:** A culture of assessment must be part of any culture of collaboration, and commitments to evaluating the effects and outcomes of collaborative interventions reinforce both major professional themes in the field of student affairs and one of the fundamental premises of all academic disciplines.

CONCLUSION

Learning Reconsidered is an introduction to new ways of understanding and supporting learning and development as intertwined, inseparable elements of the student experience. It advocates for transformative education—a holistic process of learning that places the student at the center of the learning experience. That process demands collaboration, and collaboration demands cultural change.

Sometimes cultural change and collaboration are forced by the loss of resources; it is, however, also possible to create them in response to opportunities. Reasonable caution and professional optimism are both needed attitudes as collaboration begins.

CHAPTER 10
IMPLEMENTING PROMISING PRACTICES

Coordinated by Gwendolyn Jordan Dungy
and Richard P. Keeling

With Contributions by Members of the
Partner Organizations

INTRODUCTION

Victor Hugo, the French novelist and poet, famously said, "Nothing is more powerful than an idea whose time has come." Now, early in this new century, the time has come for student affairs, in all its various disciplines, to vigorously support the idea (and conviction) that student learning is the broadly shared responsibility of all campus educators, based on the recognition that transformative learning always occurs in the active context of students' lives.

Perennially, student affairs professionals have desired and sought collaboration and tried to build partnerships with faculty to enhance and reinforce student learning. However, until *Learning Reconsidered* was published, individual student affairs professionals often had difficulty articulating the specific learning outcomes that our work would support. Since its publication, thousands of educators have used the concepts and general guidelines in *Learning Reconsidered* as a way to describe how our work can contribute to developing and achieving specific learning outcomes pertinent to the desired competencies of baccalaureate graduates.

In this chapter, we present examples from members of the Association of College and University Housing Officers–International (ACUHO-I), Association of College Unions–International (ACUI), National Association for Campus Activities (NACA), National Academic Advising Association (NACADA), and National Intramural-Recreational Sports

Association (NIRSA) that illustrate how the work of professionals in housing, college unions, campus activities, academic advising, and intramural and recreational sports contribute to a campus-wide focus on the student experience and to developing and achieving institutional learning outcomes. Members of these associations on many campuses contributed examples of successful programs and submitted responses to two broad questions:

1. What are you doing that has an impact on educating students or student learning?

2. Where are the points of collaboration or the potentials for intersection beyond your unit?

In the limited space available in this document, we can include only a few of the many programs, activities, and other examples submitted; more examples will be available in the Web-based version of *Learning Reconsidered 2: Implementing a Campus-Wide Focus on the Student Experience*. Although the wealth of material available might inspire the creation of a kind of catalogue listing the submissions, we will use some of the central themes of *Learning Reconsidered* as an organizational framework within which to present the examples.

MAKING THE WHOLE CAMPUS A LEARNING COMMUNITY

One of the most central and salient messages of *Learning Reconsidered* is that we can—and should—consider the whole campus a learning community; in Chapter 3, Borrego addresses the mapping of learning across campus and emphasizes its multi-centric, highly distributed character.

Efforts to locate learning in every part of campus and in every aspect of students' experience are illustrated by these examples:

Partnerships in the Design and Construction of the North Quad Residential and Academic Complex at the University of Michigan

This unique complex is expected to further strengthen the university's focus on blending the residential and academic life of students and to serve as a magnet for the undergraduate experience. In the planning process, representatives from the School of Information, Screen Arts and Culture Department, Communication Studies Department, and Language Resource Center will partner with University Housing to design workgroups, technology teams, building committees, and a project management team to plan a facility that will achieve the university's vision of a vibrant, technologically rich living and learning environment (submitted by Carole Henry, Director of University Housing).

Campus Learning Communities: the Residential Nexus at Central Washington University

The residential nexus is a new paradigm for the role of housing and residence education staff (Klippenstein & James, 2002).

- *Living/learning centers* are specialized residential programs that have direct connections with a specific academic program. Typically, very strong partnerships are formed between an academic program and the residence staff; faculty maintain office hours in the residence hall, classes are taught in the building, and programming efforts are focused around an academic theme or major. Examples of such centers include honors programs; programs for women in math, science, and engineering majors; and pre-med programs.

- *Theme Housing* programs offer opportunities for students with special interests to live and work together. Residential staff members are the key sponsors of these programs, but

receive significant support from academic and student affairs colleagues. Such programs include Wellness Halls, Leadership Halls, International Halls, and Substance-Free Halls.

- *Residential Learning Communities* are first-year experience programs that work toward integrating freshmen and, at times, transfer students into campus life.

(Submitted by Stacy Klippenstein, Director, University Housing and New Student Programs, Central Washington University and Co-Chair, ACUHO-I Academic Initiative Committee.)

Honors Residential College at the University of Florida

Honors Residential College at Hume Hall, is the first honors residential college designed and constructed specifically for honors students in the United States. Faculty involvement was at the foundation of this project, beginning the day the architect was selected. The associate provost, who was also the director of the university honors program committed time, money and staff in return for having a voice in the design, construction, staffing, assignments, and the use of the facility. This truly collaborative effort was initiated by housing staff members. The result of the partnership was a facility with two faculty offices, one faculty apartment, two level four classrooms (technologically enhanced), and continued faculty involvement with hall programming, hall governance and advising, policies and procedures, and a general investment in the residential college by faculty. (Provided by J. Diane "DP" Porter, Assistant Director of Housing for Academic Initiatives, University of Florida.)

Constructing Effective Learning Environments, University of Wyoming

By constructing learning linkages, housing and residence life programs position themselves to create opportunities for students to relate knowledge from the classroom to their out-of-class experiences.

- *Linking learning in different environments:* Residence Life partnered with a faculty senate committee by encouraging all resident assistants to read the campus common reading experience book and lead discussion groups in their halls. Also, Housing established themes for move-in programming to correspond with the book, and residence hall programs were created to support ideas generated from the readings.

- *Cross-cultural dining and learning:* To help resident students learn about different cultures, Residence Life partnered with Dining Services to build learning themes into menu planning. Working with international student groups, members of the Dining staff learned about foods in other cultures and produced authentic menus, linked with programs, that made dining halls part of the learning environment. (Provided by Beth McCuskey, Director of Residence Life & Dining Services, University of Wyoming.)

Creating a Learning Outcomes Based Workplace for Student Employees, University of North Dakota

The Memorial Union offers an eight-session course for staff members (including front-line supervisors, program coordinators, administrative and clerical positions, and student managers) to help departments create a learning environment for student employees using the ideas and concepts in *Learning Reconsidered*. Employment goals go beyond job satisfaction to include support of student learning. The course is designed to help employers understand and assess what students are learning on the job and how they are increasing their core skills. The objective is for the work environment to become an integrated part of the education and preparation of the whole student and of the campus learning community. The course also benefits staff members by helping them to better understand what a learning outcomes-

based environment is and how students can benefit from this type of experience and provides staff with supervisory techniques that they can use to help students learn and develop beyond the practical aspects of their jobs.

Desired learning outcomes of the course include:

1. Learn ways to identify desired learning outcomes for student employee positions using principles outlined in *Learning Reconsidered.*

2. Use assessment methods to measure how student employee behavior changes.

3. Use feedback, coaching and mentoring techniques to help student employees make connections between job tasks and learning outcomes.

4. Attain a basic understanding of how students learn.

Learning outcomes for the course were identified using the results of a survey about how student employees perceive their employment experience and what they think they are learning. (Submitted by Tony Trimarco, Director, Memorial Union, University of North Dakota)

Other Campus Programs Linking Learning Outcomes with Student Employment

- *University of Hawaii:* In addition to regular three-credit courses in leadership education and interpersonal development and non-credit workshops on personal and interpersonal development topics, coaching and advising sessions for student employees are offered (Jan Javinar, Director of Co-Curricular Activities, Programs & Services).

- *Arizona State University:* SELECT Program (Student Employees Learning, Experiencing, and Communicating Together) offers professional development workshops and discussions during the fall and spring semesters, but is just one component of a comprehensive, intentional training and development program for student employees of Student Development and Memorial Union. Specific learning outcomes for the program are currently being identified within the context of those outlined in *Learning Reconsidered*. An initiative to begin assessing student learning outcomes and the impact of training programs such as employee orientation and SELECT will be implemented as a pilot in spring of 2006 (submitted by Linda Sullivan, Assistant Director, Student Development & Memorial Union).

- *Intramural Offices:* Student employment opportunities through intramural offices allow students to learn and apply skills such as conflict resolution, working with others, dealing with difficult people, and diversity, as well as time management skills. In addition, various trainings are conducted on topics such as: sexual harassment, customer service, blood borne pathogens, emergency procedures, fire safety, first aid, cardiopulmonary resuscitation (CPR), automated external defibrillation (AED), and others. Although these skills are job-related, they are also transferable life skills that will serve students well in future endeavors. Some NIRSA members also develop and assess learning outcomes for student employee trainings and staff meetings.

- *Supervisory Skills:* Student supervisors in intramural and recreational sports programs are taught how to supervise other students. Specific trainings involve communication skills, leadership management, public speaking, listening skills, motivation, ethics, organizational skills, time management, customer service, resume writing, assertiveness/delegation, empowerment, stress reduction, and job interview skills.

Learning Through Student Activities at Hendrix College

Hendrix College uses a variety of student activities to support learning across campus. Examples include:

- *Poetry Slam:* Educating students in areas of creative writing and artistic expression through the use of stage performances.

- *College Bowl:* Competition encourages group study sessions in preparation and promotes academic advancement and achievement.

- *Leadership programs:* Students are able to earn up to two academic credits for their participation.

- *Civic responsibility:* All events associated with learning about civic responsibility questions, from copyright to scheduling and conflict resolution. (Submitted by Dave Wagner, Director of Student Activities).

Co-Curricular Planning and Learning at Frederick Community College

The college recently reorganized under three areas: Learning, Learning Support, and Administration; Student Life now reports to Learning. A co-curricular planning team—representing a diverse faculty and staff base from Learning and Learning Support—plans and implements co-curricular learning activities that are discipline-specific, contain measurable learning outcomes, and target learning areas highlighted in AAC&U's *Greater Expectations* document. Examples include a college-wide field trip to Washington, D.C., with faculty designing appropriate discipline-specific tours for the excursion; monthly "difficult dialogues" on a variety of contemporary issues; the creation of a co-curricular calendar that invites collaboration from all disciplines; and theme-focused campus activities and discussions, with multiple-discipline input (submitted by Jeanni Winston-Muir, Director of Student Life).

Cinema and Controversy at Arizona State University

Student Development and the Memorial Union collaborate with faculty members in English to organize and present *Films That Talk and Testify*; in this program, students view films—usually controversial ones—to help facilitate a meaningful dialogue (submitted by Linda Sullivan, Assistant Director, Student Development & Memorial Union).

Leadership and Learning at Boise State University

The Boise State University Student Union offers specific activities organized to address learning domains in *Learning Reconsidered:*

- *Cognitive Complexity:* Academic leadership classes incorporating service learning, Leadership Workshops, and Leadership Conferences.

- *Knowledge acquisition, integration and application:* Anticipated Leadership Studies minor and service learning incorporated in leadership development courses.

- *Humanitarianism:* Inter-group dialogues at the Student Leader Summit to enhance intercultural communication and respect; service learning incorporated in Leadership Development classes that facilitate interaction between student volunteers and clients in different cultures.

- *Civic Engagement:* Service learning in Leadership Courses, Leadership Conferences, Student Leader Summits, and leadership classes through the Leadership Program.

- *Interpersonal and Intrapersonal:* Peer leaders in the Leadership Program, leadership class project groups and discussion groups, and student groups represented at the Student Leader Summit.

- *Practical Competence:* Learning life-long leadership skills that will be useful in careers, family, or any setting through leadership courses, conferences, and involvement in Volunteer Services Board.

- *Persistence and Academic Achievement:* Mentoring student leaders in leadership development and co-curricular as well as academic achievements; validating student leader efforts through recognition programs such as the Founders' Leadership Society, Leadership Scholarships and Awards (submitted by Mahi Takazawa, Student Activities Program Coordinator).

Learning and the Fine Arts at Newberry College

As part of the liberal arts educational experience at Newberry, students are required to attend 24 fine art and lecture events (submitted by Jennifer Withers).

SUPPORTING STUDENT LEARNING AND ACADEMIC ACHIEVEMENT

Learning Reconsidered emphasizes that student affairs professionals are educators whose work complements and extends classroom learning and contributes to a whole-campus curriculum in preparing students as integrated people. The following programs and activities are examples of ways in which student affairs educators support student learning and promote academic achievement and retention.

Academic Residential Programs at Central Washington University

As a component of the university's *Residential Nexus* initiative, these programs provide academic support services to selected student groups through strong partnerships between academic affairs and student affairs staff. The residential setting is an ideal location for providing academic advising, career planning and placement, tutoring, student group formation; and programming in study skills, time management, and library usage. Since the services of many campus departments are required, coordination and collaboration among a variety of academic affairs, student affairs, and residence life constituents is essential (submitted by Stacy Klippenstein, Director, University Housing and New Student Programs).

Major Selection in the First Year at the University of Florida

The university created a new position to aid students in choosing a major during their first year of college. In response to a university goal aimed at helping students get on track early in their academic career, the Department of Housing and Residence Education submitted a proposal for this new position that targeted exploratory students living in the residence halls. The position, called a residential exploratory advisor, was jointly funded by the Department of Housing and Residence Education, the College of Agricultural and Life Sciences, the College of Liberal Arts and Sciences, and the university provost's office. This position provides an extension of the services of academic units into the residence halls, which is another bridge from housing in support of the academic mission of the university (submitted by J. Diane Porter, Assistant Director of Housing for Academic Initiatives).

Systems of Academic Support at the University of Wyoming

At the University of Wyoming, two initiatives provide academic support for students through Residence Life:

- *Minimum credit hours:* Partnering with the registrar's office, Residence Life monitors students who drop below a certain threshold of credit hours and meets with them to discuss their academic progress. Residence Life refers students to campus resources based on those meetings and the students' individual needs.

- *Learning Resource Network (LeaRN):* Residence Life collaborates in this program, the purpose of which is to provide systems of support for the first two years of college, including support in and outside the classroom. Residence Life participates on the advisory board for LeaRN and has partnered in a variety of programs to provide student academic support including a review of tutoring resources, grass roots initiatives to bring speakers to campus, and developing new initiatives to bring faculty into the residence halls and dining center (submitted by Beth McCuskey, Director of Residence Life & Dining Services).

ACUI Regional Conference as Professional Development for Students, University of North Dakota

Student managers are given the opportunity to attend regional ACUI conferences. Before attending the conferences, students are given an instruction sheet that explains that this is a special privilege for professional development and networking with other staff and student leaders from unions throughout the region. They are expected to share ideas and experiences as well as attend educational sessions to improve their personal and professional skills. When they return from the conference, students are required to submit a reflection paper with responses to several short answer questions to the director of the Memorial Union. Examples of the questions include:

1. Describe how this conference improved your overall supervisory and management skills.

2. What did you learn that you can apply to your personal life and how could you benefit from it?

3. Describe two-to-three ideas you learned that could be applied to your particular service area or the Memorial Union as a whole; how would we benefit from these new ideas (program or service)? (Submitted by Tony Trimarco, Director, Memorial Union)

Practicum and Internship Opportunities in Intramural-Recreational Sports

Intramural and recreational sports programs provide practicum and internship opportunities for masters and doctoral degree students in assessment and research studies. In return, the academic departments develop training related to learning outcomes and assessment and present them to our staff and assist the intramural and recreational sports programs in developing assessments and conducting and analyzing research.

Linking Academic Advising to Learning Outcomes

The National Academic Advising Association (NACADA) has worked with the advising community to assist in the development and assessment of student learning outcomes for academic advising across the institution. Sample institutions that have made significant progress in this area are:

- *College of DuPage:* A three-year project focusing on advising and student learning was undertaken as a major component of this community college's quality improvement process. The outcome of the project is a clearly defined set of knowledge competencies for students that are taught through advising experiences. In addition to mapping the competencies to the student's academic progression, specific quantitative and qualitative measures are utilized to measure the student's achievement of these knowledge competencies.

- *University of Louisville:* A cross-institutional team has worked for two years to develop a clear vision and mission for academic advising and student learning outcomes across the university. These outcomes provide a focused curriculum for advising, primarily in the freshman and sophomore years, that is taught in a variety of means and formats. The team has further developed several assessment strategies that are both qualitative and quantitative as utilize both direct and indirect measures.

- *University of Arkansas-Fayetteville:* A two-year project has resulted in the development of university-level learning outcomes including advising outcomes. The university student-learning outcomes for academic advising have been developed to clearly respect the decentralized advising model in which each college is responsible for the teaching and measurement of these student-learning outcomes for the students in that college.

- *Ivy Tech Community College-Indianapolis:* As part of a three-year grant from the Lumina Foundation, this comprehensive college has been in the process of restructuring its academic advising experiences for students to tie them directly to a strong mission and a set of student learning outcomes. The college is focusing on developing strategies for the development, achievement, and documentation of the student learning outcomes for the diverse student populations on this urban campus.

INNOVATIONS IN STUDENT LEARNING

These programs are examples of innovative or entrepreneurial efforts by student affairs educators to design student learning experiences that engage and inspire students.

Last Lecture Program, Arizona State University

In the Last Lecture Series, designed and supported by Student Development & Memorial Union, professors are nominated by students to compete to write and deliver a lecture as if it were the last lecture they would ever give (submitted by Linda Sullivan, Assistant Director).

Student-Faculty Retreat, Arizona State University

The Student-Faculty Retreat offers interactive team-building activities that challenge faculty and students to identify ways to communicate better, build stronger relationships, and have a more successful experience in the classroom, with post-retreat evaluations allowing students to reflect on the experience.

Scholars 4 Success Program, University of Missouri-Kansas City

The Scholars 4 Success Program links student and academic affairs in providing a dedicated learning support program for scholarship students.

LEAD Program, University of Southern California

USC LEAD is a leadership program that includes workshops, seminars, a mentor program, and the Emerging Leaders Program. The student staff engages in learning as they create and implement the activities and programs. They challenge themselves to be more knowledgeable so they may pass on the most accurate information to their peers through weekly workshops on a variety of leadership topics. The notable innovation in the program is that each year, a theme is chosen as the programming foundation; in the current academic year, it is ethics. Speakers and discussions are planned around this theme to further stimulate learning, and Campus Activities asked other departments both within and outside of Student Affairs to collaborate on ethics programs in support of USC LEAD (submitted by Heather Larabee, Director of Campus Activities).

POINTS OF COLLABORATION

The Boise State University Student Union illustrates in its programming the many opportunities that student affairs educators have for collaboration. Mahi Takazawa, Student Activities Program Coordinator, submitted this list of their collaborative projects:

- *Academic Advising (to encourage advisees to enroll in Leadership classes),*

- *Alumni Association (to obtain support from student leader alumni),*

- *Career Services (career development of current student leaders),*

- *Service Learning (to instill an ethic of life-long service and civic engagement),*

- *Cultural Center (Diversity Workshops),*

- *Women's Center (Gender Workshops),*

- *Community non-profits (to instill an ethic of life-long service and civic engagement),*

- *Residence Life (to build a community of leaders),*

- *Health, Wellness, and Counseling (to maintain the sanity and good health of students),*

- *Campus Recreation (outdoor programs to learn group leadership skills),*

- *Admissions (recruiting future college student leaders from high school),*

- *Orientation (to promote leadership and volunteer programs to new students),*

- *Athletics (to work with student athlete leaders, especially from Student Athlete Advisory Committee), and*

- *Academic colleges and departments (interdisciplinary Leadership Studies minor and electives, volunteer and awareness programs)*

COLLABORATION IN TEACHING

Student affairs educators in every area are effective teaching partners in academic courses (especially, first-year transition and seminar courses). Examples of collaborative teaching include:

Support of Students in Learning Projects

Educators in college unions, campus activities, intramural-recreational sports, academic advising, housing and residence life, and many other departments in student affairs work with many undergraduate and graduate students who are doing class projects, research (especially undergraduate research), internships, or service learning.

Teaching in Freshman Transition, Freshman Seminar, and University 101 Courses

In preparing this volume, the authors received submissions describing the participation of student affairs educators in freshman transition, freshman/first-year seminar, and university 101 courses from colleagues in more than 20 institutions, including, among many others, Hendrix College, the State University of New York at Suffolk, and St. Norbert College.

Specialty Teaching in Intramural-Recreational Sports

Staff members in Wellness Centers have collaborated with the departments of Physical Therapy and Physical Education and Exercise Science on their campuses in the development and presentation of several academic classes, such as Professional Skills in Personal Training and Fundamentals of Group Exercise. Personal Training courses may be taught through the Department of Physical Therapy or other academic departments to provide doctoral students with valuable skills to enhance their future careers.

CONCLUSION

The examples presented in this chapter offer only a limited snapshot of the initiatives and opportunities that student affairs professionals have identified to collaborate in the work of learning on their campuses. What J. Diane Porter, assistant director of housing for academic initiatives at the University of Florida, wrote regarding the participation of Housing in these activities is true more generally of other student affairs departments and programs as well:

The keys to the success of each of these examples have been commitment, communication, research to provide the rationale for a program, willingness to take a risk, and innovation. Each was created in support of the academic mission of the institution and with the idea of helping students succeed. Each example has broadened the influence of housing to the greater campus community and, in turn, educated housing staff in regard to other areas of the institution.

Jeanni Winston-Muir, director of student life at Frederick Community College, summarizes these opportunities as follows:

Emphasis is on the role of student life in learning as the "laboratory" experience that supports the in-class discipline learning; we provide an environment of sheltered risk that enables students to apply and practice what they have learned in the classroom to real life situations. We are the bridge between knowledge and application and expected competence upon graduation.

Intramural and recreational sports professionals point out that research in their field has identified a relationship between participation and several learning outcomes, including the ability to adjust to new job demands, working cooperatively in a group, understanding graphic information, and defining and solving problems (Smith, 1988-89). They add that literally everything done in their programs, facilities, and services enhances student learning through learning lifelong skills, wellness, fitness, and functioning in a workplace. In addition, encouraging faculty to participate in intramural and club sport activities allows the students the opportunity to experience interaction with faculty outside of the classroom.

In the coming years, the number, diversity, and adaptability of examples like all of the ones presented in this chapter will continue to grow as more student affairs professionals develop clever and scalable ways to give life to the definition of learning proposed in *Learning Reconsidered:* "A complex, holistic, multi-centric activity that occurs throughout and across the college experience" (p. 5).

REFERENCES

Abes, E. & Jones, S. (2004) Meaning-making capacity and the dynamics of lesbian college students' multiple dimensions of identity. *Journal of College Student Development* 45, 612-632.

American Association of Higher Education, American College Personnel Association, & National Association of Student Personnel Administrators (1998) *Powerful partnerships: a shared responsibility for learning.* Washington, DC: authors.

American College Personnel Association (1994) The student learning imperative: implications for student affairs. Washington, DC: author. Also available at www.acpa.nche.edu/sli/sli.htm.

American College Personnel Association & National Association of Student Personnel Administrators (1997) *Principles of good practice for student affairs.* Available at www.acpa.nche.edu/pgp/principle.htm.

American College Personnel Association & National Association of Student Personnel Administrators (2004) *Learning Reconsidered: A Campus-Wide Focus on the Student Experience.* Washington, DC: authors. Available at www.naspa.org and www.acpa.nche.edu.

American Council on Education (1937) The student personnel point of view. Washington, DC: author.

Anderson, W. (1997) *The future of the self: Inventing the post-modern person.* New York, NY: Jeremy Tarcher/Putnam Books.

Argyris, C. (1982) *Reasoning, learning and action.* San Francisco: Jossey Bass.

Astin, A.W. & associates (2003) 9 principles of good practice in assessing student learning. Washington, DC: American Association for Higher Education.

Barr, R. B., & Tagg, J. (1995) From Teaching to Learning—A New Paradigm for Undergraduate Education. *Change* 27(6),12–25.

Baxter Magolda, M. B. (1998) Developing self-authorship in young adult life. *Journal of College Student Development, 39*(2). 143-155.

Baxter Magolda, M. B. (1999) Defining and redefining student learning. In E. Whitt (Ed.) *Student learning as student affairs work.* NASPA Monograph Series no. 23, pp 35-49. Washington, DC: National Association of Student Personnel Administrators.

Baxter Magolda, M.B. (1999) *Creating contexts for learning and self-authorship.* Nashville, TN: Vanderbilt University Press.

Baxter Magolda, M. B. (Ed.) (2000) *Teaching to promote intellectual and personal maturity: Incorporating students' worldviews and identities into the learning process* (New Directions for Teaching and Learning, No. 82). San Francisco: Jossey-Bass.

Baxter Magolda, M. B. (2001) *Making their own way: Narratives for transforming higher education to promote self-development.* Sterling, VA: Stylus Publishing.

Baxter Magolda, M. B. (2003) Identity and learning: Student affairs' role in transforming higher education. *Journal of College Student Development, 44,* 231-247.

Baxter Magolda, M. B., & King, P. M. (Eds) (2004) *Learning partnerships: Theory and models of practice to educate for self-authorship.* Sterling, VA: Stylus Press.

Bloland, PA., Stamatakos, L.C., & Rogers, R.R. (1994) *Reform in student affairs: A critique of student development.* Greensboro, NC: ERIC Counseling and Student Services Clearinghouse.

Bloom B. S. (1956) *Taxonomy of Educational Objectives, Handbook I: The Cognitive Domain.* New York: David McKay Co Inc.

Boyer, E.L. (1987) *College: The undergraduate experience in America.* New York: Harper & Row.

Brown, R. (1972). *Student development in tomorrow's higher education: a return to the academy.* Washington, DC: American Personnel and Guidance Association.

Caine, R. Caine, G, McClintic, C. & Klimek, K. (2005) *Brain/mind learning principles in action.* Thousand Oaks, CA: Corwin Press.

Dolence, M., & Norris, D. (1995) *Transforming Higher Education.* Ann Arbor, MI: Society for College and University Planning.

Foucalt, M. (1970) *The order of things.* New York, NY: Random House.

Foucalt, M. (1980) *Power/knowledge.* New York, NY: Pantheon Books.

Fried, J., & associates (1995) *Shifting paradigms in student affairs: Culture, context, meaning, and learning.* Lanham, MD: American College Personnel Association/University Press of America.

Friere, P. (1990) *Pedagogy of the oppressed.* NY: Continuum Books.

Giroux, H. (1992) *Border crossings: Cultural workers and the politics of education.* New York, NY: Routledge, Chapman, and Hall.

Gordon, V. N. & Habley, W. R. (2000) *Academic advising: A comprehensive handbook.* San Francisco: Jossey-Bass.

Greater Expectations National Panel (2002) *Greater expectations: a new vision for learning as a nation goes to college.* Washington, DC: Association of American Colleges and Universities (www.aacu.org). Complete text available at www.greaterexpectations.org.

Hamrick, F. A., Evans, N. J., & Schuh, J. H. (2002) *Foundations of student affairs practice: How philosophy, theory, and research strengthen educational outcomes.* San Francisco: Jossey-Bass.

Hooks, b. (1994) *Teaching to transgress.* NY: Routledge Press.

Hooks, b. (2003) *Teaching community.* NY: Routledge Press.

Jernstedt, G. (2005) *Learning, teaching and the brain.* Hanover, NH: Dartmouth College.

Jones, S., & McEwen, M. (2000) A conceptual model of multiple dimensions of identity. *Journal of College Student Development* 45, 405-414.